Vertex: The Third Angle

Donna Henson

ISBN: 0-86690-543-X

First Published by:
ONLINE College of Astrology

First Electronic Edition:2002

First Printed Edition: 2003

Published by:
American Federation of Astrologers, Inc.
6535 S. Rural Road
Tempe AZ 85283

Printed in the United States of America

Acknowledgements

Many people have helped in researching and gathering information for this book. First, I want to acknowledge the 30 people of the Vertex research group, which met while the North Texas Chapter of NCGR had its brief lifetime. They are: Sylvia Andrews, Robert Boehler, Ray Bryant, Gail Carswell, Joanne Drake, Michael Foltz, Kay Fowler, Frances Garrett, David Gates, Cynthia Harr, Donna Henson, Lydia Hunt, Cheryl Johnson, Iris Kinney, Micki Kleinsmith, Karen Kovak, Alice McFarlen, Shannon O'Neill, Dee Pastor, Susie Patterson, Diana Rivere, Elaine Russey, Hugh Sims, Roy Snell, Teresa Thompson, Sona Vaughn, Lynn Walters, Sandra Williams, and Kaye Wilson.

I especially want to thank Michael Foltz and my brother, Alan Barnes, whose help with the computer was invaluable. Also, I thank all the subjects of the 60 interviews, many of whom are members of the Astrological Society of Fort Worth, friends, and students. Special thanks goes to Lynn Walters who helped develop the research model, Gail Carswell who helped with proof reading the database material, and Ray Bryant whose insights were especially helpful.

I also thank Dr. Zipporah Dobyns for introducing me to this important point in astrology and to Doris Greaves of Australia whose encouragement in completing the project inspired the work. Finally, my husband, George, whose patience and support while this was being produced, made it possible.

Contents

Preface

A few years after World War II Charles Jayne and L.E. Johndro discovered the Vertex. At the same time it was discovered in Germany where its two ends were known as the Eos and Hespera points. It is called an angle of fate, yet not of an event that must occur, but one that will occur only if the person has set up a chain reaction of actions that must lead to a certain result. If the previous action is changed or modified, the events set off by Vertex activations are changed or modified too. Its actions come through or with other people since it is always on the right (west) side of the chart.

Dr. Zipporah Dobyns has likened the Vertex to the seventh and tenth houses and its opposite point, the AntiVertex to the 1st and 4th houses. Virginia Reyer has said it indicates "events likely to come to pass despite efforts to avoid them."

While it is the point that is the intersection of the Ecliptic with the Prime Vertical, all sensitive points (excluding midpoints, Arabic Parts, etc.) are either planets or nodes. Like the Moon's Nodes, the Vertex and AntiVertex are nodes. An aspect to one is also an aspect to the other. For example, a trine to the Vertex is also a sextile to the AntiVertex or a sextile to the Vertex is also a trine to the AntiVertex.

Zip Dobyns, at a workshop she gave in Fort Worth for the Astrological Society of Fort Worth, first brought the Vertex to my attention in the early 1970s. Since I had recently had two strong progressions of the Vertex to a natal planet and an angle in my chart, I had to know more about this very important point. I began using it in all the charts I did, but since they were calculated by hand in those days, this was not a large number of them. Besides taking as much time to calculate as the Ascendant, I soon learned that one could not estimate its movement year by year in secondary progressions since it was very erratic. It seemed to slow down and speed up in kind of a bell curve over a period of many years.

Then came computers! This opened up many possibilities for researching the effects of the Vertex. I began observing the effects of sextiles, trines, quincunxes, and squares as well as the stronger conjunctions and oppositions.

In 1992, I met Doris Greaves of Australia through a mutual friend and learned that she too was doing an ongoing research of the Vertex using Cosmobiology, which uses the hard aspects. In 1994, she asked me to do a book with her on the Vertex. She went on to publish her findings in her 1999 book *Regulus Ebertin Cosmobiology Beyond 2000* as well as several articles and lectures on the subject.

I was much slower, but that same year Michael Foltz, a Fort Worth astrologer and computer expert, and I started a research group with a short-lived NCGR chapter in this area. Nearly 25 people worked in the group, first studying the few articles and publications on the subject and then doing carefully constructed interviews of one to four hours each in length with nearly 60 people to see what had happened with each of the Ptolemaic aspects and the quincunx during their lives. This data was put into a database, and much of it is the basis for what I've done in this book.

I have tried to present some of the possibilities for using the Vertex. Most of my work has been with secondary progressions. Doris Greaves has ably demonstrated the Vertex's use with solar arc directions and midpoints in Cosmobiology. Its use in rectification for me has been invaluable. It is also highly significant in charts of important events and in solar returns. Then Kaye Shinker's work with conjunctions to the Vertex in the natal chart, financial astrology and synastry alerted me to these areas. Also, transits of outer planets to the Vertex and eclipses are areas that are ripe for more research.

Donna Henson

1

To Whet Your Appetite

I was asked by a friend to do a short health and vocational reading for his wife. The chart (see Chart 1) was prepared, but since she is a busy professional artist, we have been unable to get together for the reading. However, when I saw her husband just before the two

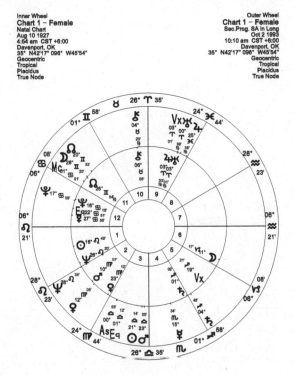

took one of their many long trips, I mentioned that she had one or two major events coming up very soon pertaining to a foreign country or a university. On this trip she was approached to speak about her style of art at Oxford University in England and was given an offer, expenses paid, to go to Africa for a month to paint. What indicated these big dual events? Her Vertex by secondary progression was **conjunct the very close conjunction (3 Aries 01 and 3 Aries 03) of Jupiter and Uranus** in her ninth house of foreign countries and universities.

My brother (see Chart 2) also had an aspect of his **progressed Vertex to a ninth house planet** a few years ago. He was contacted by a member of the Supreme Court who had been told that my brother was "as much of an expert as anyone" on Texas education reforms.

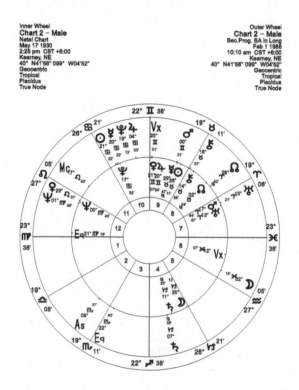

2

While these two examples are quite favorable, not all Vertex aspects are so. One person had the progressed Vertex **conjunct his sixth house Jupiter** (which rules his fifth of entertainment) when he and the rock group he was a part of made a CD that was very successful. The group had not had that kind of success before or since. The same person had had a Vertex **conjunction with his natal Venus** several years earlier (see Chart 3). At that time he had to have an emergency tracheotomy (Venus—the throat).

Another young man had progressed **Vertex in the ninth house conjunct Uranus in the sign Cancer** (see Chart 4). Uranus rules his fourth house, and at this time he bought his first home. Several years later when the progressed Vertex was **square his natal Saturn** and the progressed **Midheaven was square his natal Vertex**, he divorced and had to sell the house (Saturn is co-ruler of his fourth house).

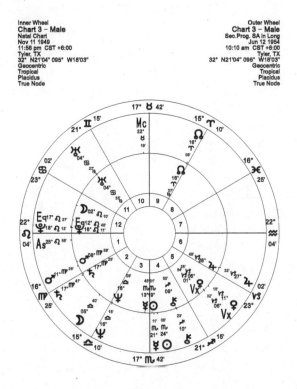

I have the charts of several people who have either divorced (if married) or married (if single) when the Vertex **progressed to the seventh house cusp.** Since the Vertex always falls on the western side of the chart, most people will have either this conjunction if the Vertex is natally in the fourth, fifth, or sixth houses or a conjunction of the Vertex with the Midheaven if the Vertex is in the seventh, eighth, or ninth houses. This conjunction can also work in other ways.

This occurred in the chart of one man who insisted that "nothing" had happened at the time the progressed Vertex made the **conjunction to the cusp of the seventh.** There were no marriage problems, but knowing that these conjunctions are often some of the strongest progressions of a person's lifetime, I asked him again three years later. This time he told me that this was the time he and his wife learned that their son was on drugs, a fact that made their

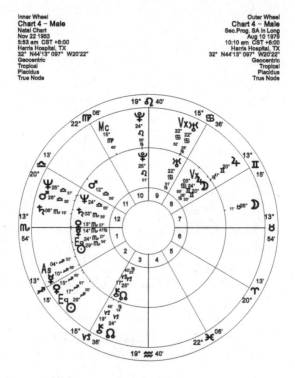

Inner Wheel
Chart 4 – Male
Natal Chart
Nov 22 1953
5:53 am CST +6:00
Harris Hospital, TX
32° N44'13" 097° W20'22"
Geocentric
Tropical
Placidus
True Node

Outer Wheel
Chart 4 – Male
Sec.Prog. SA In Long
Aug 10 1979
10:10 am CST +6:00
Harris Hospital, TX
32° N44'13" 097° W20'22"
Geocentric
Tropical
Placidus
True Node

Inner Wheel
Chart 5 – Female
Natal Chart
Jul 7 1954
1:32 pm CST +6:00
Waco, TX
31° N32'57" 097° W08'47"
Geocentric
Tropical
Placidus
True Node

Middle Wheel
Chart 5 – Female
Sec.Prog. SA In Long
Jan 18 2000
10:10 am CST +6:00
Waco, TX
31° N32'57" 097° W08'47"
Geocentric
Tropical
Placidus
True Node

True Node
Placidus
Tropical
Geocentric
31° N32'57" 097° W08'47"
Waco, TX
10:10 am CST +6:00
Jan 18 2000
Directed – Solar Arc
Chart 5 – Female

life a nightmare for several years. He simply could not talk about the event near the time it happened. This was a strong event that he had to work out with another person. Natally, Scorpio was on the cusp of his fifth of children with its ruler, Pluto, semi-square Neptune, which rules drugs. His other two sons are a photographer (Neptune) and a musician (Neptune).

A recent example was found January 18, 2000, when a 45-year-old client (see Chart 5) came to me saying she needed some hope for her life, which had become very drab. She lived with her elderly father and did not have a good relationship with him. She was unable to work due to a bi-polar condition, which had resisted treatment.

The woman was divorced and had lost custody of her son because she was not able to take care of him. Besides all of that, she was trying to get a disability allowance from Social Security and, so far, had been denied. She wanted to know when her life would get better.

Ordinarily, that situation would take some deep analysis, but, having studied her chart, I told her not to worry. Her life was going to change drastically and her problems would be solved very soon-not through her own effort. Clients often hope the astrologer will tell them something like this, but in real life, problems usually do not solve themselves in the way I expected hers to do. Why could I say this to her?

She had the progressed Vertex in the ninth conjunct her natal Uranus (sudden events). That is a very strong progression, but in addition to that, she also had her **directed Vertex almost exactly conjunct her natal Midheaven** (her position in the world and her father). As if that weren't enough, in three days the January 21, 2000 **lunar eclipse would also be conjunct her Midheaven (0 Leo 28).**

The first week after the reading, nothing happened, but during the seven days of the second week, her father fell and broke his hip. He had surgery for the hip. The next day he had a heart attack and died while in the hospital. Her social security disability came through during those seven days, and an inheritance will come to her from her father. To make things even better for her, she met a new boyfriend at the grocery store, and when I talked to her last, she told me they were talking about marriage. Needless to say, her health is much better, and her psychiatrist says he is amazed at the improvement she's had.

Other aspects from or to the Vertex give results too. **The progressed Vertex of one woman at 5 Capricorn 38 was square natal Uranus, which rules her eighth house of death.** She had been

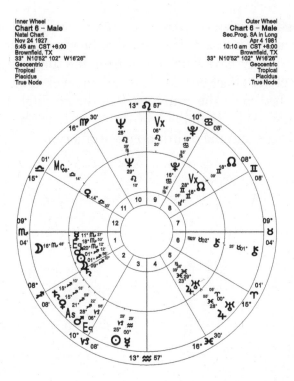

Inner Wheel
Chart 6 – Male
Natal Chart
Nov 24 1927
5:45 am CST +6:00
Brownfield, TX
33° N10'52" 102° W16'26"
Geocentric
Tropical
Placidus
True Node

Outer Wheel
Chart 6 – Male
Sec.Prog. SA in Long
Apr 4 1981
10:10 am CST +8:00
Brownfield, TX
33° N10'52" 102° W16'26"
Geocentric
Tropical
Placidus
True Node

dating a man for about three years when he died suddenly of an aneurysm. Besides the conjunction and the square I am finding results with sextiles, trines, and quincunxes as well. Other aspects probably work too, but my research was limited to these six aspects.

While these Vertex progressions usually indicate important, seemingly fated events which involve working something out with another person (western side of the chart), its opposite point, the AntiVertex, describes an event the individual causes or experiences which does not so directly involve others. This was the case with a client I had in 1981 (see Chart 6). His **progressed Mars opposed his natal Vertex (conjunct his AntiVertex)** because, like the Moon's Nodes, the Vertex and AntiVertex form a polarity.

He too insisted that "nothing" had happened. I asked him about several possibilities since progressed Mars was in the second opposing the eighth house Vertex. Finally, he blurted out that nothing could possibly have happened during the time the aspect was most strongly in effect because he had had an emergency surgery then, so he had spent the entire week in the hospital and the next two or three weeks at home recovering and, as he said, "doing nothing." (Mars and the eighth house—surgery.)

2

What Is the Vertex?

When we ask what the Vertex is, we are really asking two questions: What is the Vertex astronomically? What is the Vertex astrologically?

What Is the Vertex Astronomically?

Astronomically, the Vertex is the intersection of the Prime Vertical with the Ecliptic in the West.

There are five Great Circles:

- The Ecliptic

- The Prime Vertical

- The Meridian

- The Celestial Equator

- The Horizon

A great circle is defined as "a circle on a sphere such that the plane containing the circle passes through the center of the sphere." All of the angles come from these intersections:

- The **Vertex** is the intersection of the **Prime Vertical** and the **Ecliptic** in the West.

- The **AntiVertex (AVx)** is the intersection of the **Prime Vertical** and the **Ecliptic** in the East.

- The **Ascendant** is the intersection of the **Horizon** and the **Ecliptic** in the East.

- The **Descendant** is the intersection of the **Horizon** and the **Ecliptic** in the West.

- The **Aries Point** is the intersection of the **Ecliptic** and the **Equator** in the East.

- The **Libra Point** is the intersection of the **Ecliptic** and the **Equator** in the West.

- The **Equatorial Ascendant** (often mistakenly called the East Point) is the intersection of the **Prime Vertical** and the **Equator** in the East.

- The **Equatorial Descendant** is the intersection of the **Prime Vertical** and the **Equator** in the West.

Calculating the Vertex

1. Get the **co-latitude** by subtracting the birth latitude from 90 degrees.

2. Then take the **natal IC** (Nadir, fourth house cusp) and look it up in a tables of houses as if it were the **Midheaven**.

3. Go down the **Ascendant column** under the heading found in Step 2 to the co-latitude. The figure found here is the **Vertex**.

While the **Midheaven** can be defined as the degree of the zodiac that is either exactly **due north** or exactly **due south** of the place of birth or place of observation, the **Vertex** is defined as the point that is exactly **due west** of the place of birth or observation.

From this it can be seen that the Vertex has as much astronomical validity as any of the other angles.

How Does the Progressed Vertex Move?

The yearly movement of the progressed Vertex is very erratic. It gets faster and then slower each year in a kind of wave. For that reason, it is not easy to estimate its movement by progression. Thank goodness for computers! Most astrological computer programs will do the work of calculation for us.

In my own chart it has moved as little as 30 minutes a year to more than three degrees per year. As a result, many people have experienced the Vertex in only one or two signs while others have had the progressed Vertex in as many as four or more signs. While each aspect the progressed Vertex makes retains some association with the natal sign of the Vertex, it also picks up some characteristics of the sign(s) it has progressed to as well.

Again using my chart as an example, I was born with the Vertex in Sagittarius giving the following positions:

Age 0 to 7	Sagittarius	(7 years)
Age 7 to 35	Capricorn	(28 years)
Age 35 to 53	Aquarius	(18 years)
Age 53 to 67	Pisces	(14 years)

It has now progressed into Aries. Although much of my life has been spent in ninth house-Sagittarius activities, during the **Capricorn** period I had many duties and obligations since my mother was a single parent and I had two brothers to care for. Later in this period there was a very restrictive marriage, so the whole period could be characterized as one of struggle and limitations.

When the Vertex progressed into **Aquarius**, I divorced this husband. I was teaching in a high school, and certainly this called for dealing with all kinds of people, even those "one cannot tolerate." I had to develop detachment. When it progressed into **Pisces**, I developed several health problems, which were not solved until I changed my work to do what I really wanted to do. So, in a general way, I can see that there were different expectations of me with each sign change.

This was true of several others I talked to as well. One woman, who was born with the Vertex in **Pisces**, has always been closely associated with health fields. When her Vertex progressed into **Aries**, her family's home burned down. During this Aries period (ages three to 12), she did extremely well in school and decided to "be herself" (Aries) instead of doing what her peers expected of her, which would have meant hiding her exceptional mental gifts. From ages 12 to 23 with the Vertex in **Taurus**, she graduated from high school and college and helped her husband through medical school. When the Vertex went into **Gemini**, from ages 23 to 48, she went back to college for her Master's degree in medical technology, and she taught hematology on the college level. When the Vertex went into **Cancer**, she got into administration at a large hospital where she was in charge of the laboratories. Part of her job was to "make sure patients came first" (Cancer).

Two other women I talked to had their Vertexes in **Cancer** at birth, and, for both, it had progressed to **Leo**. Both became more assertive with these changes and both entered career fields when this occurred.

What Is the Vertex Astrologically?

The Vertex represents a role or part we play that is **not a matter of personal choice** but is fated or destined by the part we play in our world.

We **cannot really change things** signified by what is involved with the Vertex. Vertex events involve other people. They are automatic forcing "personality completion." For example, a person with the Vertex in Cancer may not be comfortable dealing with emotional or family matters until he learns to do so. Vertex events make it possible to learn this.

The Vertex represents **one's lot in life** determined by one's past. The sign the Vertex is in represents a quality one needs to bring out, i.e., with the Vertex in Aries one needs to bring out initiative and the courage to start new things and to lead.

There is a **fated quality** to things represented by the Vertex. The Sun on the Ascendant gives a personal approach to life, but one has something to say about it. Sun on the Vertex is a "key man" in a group or collective situation and very much subjected to fated situations.

Coming on the right side of the chart, it is also **a mirror to ourselves** as to how other people see us. It shows expectancies of a person as a result of the reputation he has earned.

The Ascendant is our face to the world; the Vertex tells **how the world interprets this face**. It represents the result of personal growth as it is interpreted by one's environment as a result of what a person has done.

We are left with questions. What does the Vertex add to our understanding of human nature? What does it symbolize in the chart? How does it relate to the other angles, especially the Ascendant and the Midheaven? Delphine Jay writes that "as a result of what one is (Ascendant) and what one does (Midheaven), the **Vertex represents what is expected of him**."

I once read an essay titled "Every Man's Natural Desire to Be Somebody Else" by Samuel Crothers. He says that this idea "explains why people are so often offended when we say nice things about them, and why it is that, when we say harsh things about them, they take it as a compliment."

To really know any person, including ourselves, we must know what he looks like, where he resides, and what he does for a living. But that's not enough. We must also know what he used to be, what he used to think he was, and what he used to think he ought to be and might be if he worked hard enough. Also what he might have been if things had happened otherwise. All these complexities are part of his own apprehension of himself. They are what make him so much more interesting to himself than he is to anyone else. This natural desire to be somebody else is the result of knowing that there is much more to our natures than the obvious: our present appearance, occupation, and place of residence. As Crothers said:

> The member of one profession is always flattered by being taken for a skilled practitioner of another. Try it on your minister. Instead of saying, "That was an excellent sermon of yours this morning," say "As I listened to your cogent argument, I thought what a successful lawyer you would have made." Then he will say, "I did think of taking to the law."

We like having those parts of ourselves brought out that we know are there but we have not yet developed.

Now, what does this have to do with the Vertex? The Vertex symbolizes a facet of our natures that we are compelled to bring forth when the Vertex is activated. In bringing it forth, we must remember that it has always been there. This is an area of our lives we know we could develop and will have the chance to bring out when the Vertex is activated. This compulsion to do so is what gives the Vertex a "fated" quality.

This still does not explain, though, why we bring forth one type of experience rather than another. The Vertex works somewhat like the Moon's Nodes since the Vertex and AntiVertex is also an axis. We say we have already developed the qualities of the South Node, and we get our greatest growth from the North Node. Likewise, we have well-developed qualities of the AntiVertex, and we need to bring forth the qualities of the Vertex.

What We Need to Bring Forth by Sign

The sign of the Vertex tells us what we need to bring forth. In:

- **Aries**, our ability to take initiative instead of looking to others (Libra) to do so;

- **Taurus**, to earn money for oneself rather than (Scorpio) looking to others for support;

- **Gemini**, to communicate specific facts and figures rather than (Sagittarius) abstractions;

- **Cancer**, to learn to handle emotional factors in situations rather than (Capricorn) taking an administrative role;

- **Leo**, to deal with self-esteem issues rather than (Aquarius) being a part of the masses;

- **Virgo**, to develop usefulness through practical, material insights rather than (Pisces) the emotional, psychological insights that lead to compassion;

- **Libra**, to bring opposing factions together so they may work in harmony rather than (Aries) doing the job oneself;

- **Scorpio**, to assist others pertaining to partnership security rather than (Taurus) dealing with one's own security;

- **Sagittarius**, to develop a broader vision of things rather

15

than (Gemini) relying on facts without considering the significance of these facts;

- **Capricorn,** to develop the ability to organize with caution, prudence, and patience rather than (Cancer) dealing with matters emotionally;

- **Aquarius,** to develop the idea that you are one among equals rather than (Leo) one whose feelings of superiority keep him from bothering to be a friend; and

- **Pisces,** to develop selflessness and emotional or psychological insights rather than (Virgo) the practical, material insights.

Each of these urges can be positive, but none is positive when we stay in one end of the polarity without developing the other to become a balanced, complete human being.

What We Need to Bring Forth by Planet or Angle

Just as the sign tells us what we need to bring forth, the planet or angle aspecting the Vertex tells us how we are apt to be compelled to do so. Thus, a Libra Vertex that is aspected by Saturn might be expected to bring opposing factions together patiently and cautiously (Saturn) while if the same Libra Vertex were aspected by Mars, one might use great force or action to bring opposing forces together (Mars). The aspects between these two as well as the other aspects to these two planets or points tell how harmoniously or inharmoniously this may be brought about. It also tells the consequences to the native.

What We Need to Bring Forth by House

In latitudes above 23°26', the Vertex always falls on the right (west) side of the chart. It is usually in the fifth, sixth, seventh, or eighth houses. Occasionally it is found in the fourth or the ninth houses.

When working with events in secondary progressions, the house placement of the natal position as well as the progressed one often gives us clues to the nature of the event.

When found in the **fourth house**, one deals with family, endings, security, and emotional expression. When found in the **fifth house**, one deals with his creative expression versus his individuality. In the **sixth house** one deals with practical service and idealism. In the **seventh house** a person deals with balancing his own needs with those of others. In the **eighth house** one deals with his habits (overindulgences) and his money patterns. In the **ninth house** one deals with the principles of things or legal and religious conflicts.

Two Examples

Using Ivy Goldstein-Jacobson's chart as an example, her Aquarius Vertex in the eighth house inclined her to a pursuit for the meaning of life in an unorthodox (for her day) way: astrology. The aspects to her Vertex are sextiles from Venus and the Sun in the ninth in Aries. So she initiated ideas and took opportunities to gain pleasure (Venus) and prestige (Sun) through writing and publishing (ninth house).

Another example is Jimmy Carter's chart. March and McEvers give his birth time as 7:00 a.m. giving him a Gemini Vertex, a Libra Ascendant, and a Cancer Midheaven. When the Vertex was activated, it became necessary for him to communicate clearly and concisely on issues. He needed to have facts and ideas without the philosophical abstractions (of the Sagittarius AntiVertex) that would make him appear vacillating and impossible to pin down. It was in his debates with Gerald Ford that he had to communicate factually and take a clear stand on his views with hard-core facts to win the confidence of the people.

3

The Signs of the Vertex

The sign of the Vertex tells us **what we need to develop to complete our personalities**. It will also describe the type of action you are apt to take when the Vx/AVx axis is activated.

We formed a research group through an NCGR chapter a few years ago. We wanted to show that all of the aspects we researched (conjunction, sextile, square, inconjunct, opposition) produced results. We chose to use ordinary people, members of the group, their friends, clients, and relatives rather than famous people. Due to the fact that many of these events are subtle, this gave us a chance to know the subject's attitudes and feelings about the events-information that is not usually available in biographies of the famous. In addition, as astrologers, these are the people we usually work with, and in personal interviews (of one to four hours) they often reveal parts of their lives that we never hear about among the famous.

We ran a list on the computer of all the aspects each person had had in his lifetime to or from the Vertex. We encouraged these subjects to list as many events with dates as close as possible for reference. Then we developed a questionnaire that we helped the subjects fill out on each aspect as well as each sign and house change. They were given a list of keywords for every planet, sign, house, and kind of aspect. The information we gathered was put into a database and analyzed. We completed 60 of these interviews. The number of aspects or other factors varied greatly due to the age of the subjects and the shape of the charts. Using the first 40 years only (because most subjects were in their 40's or older), the number of aspects, sign, or house changes each had varied from about 12 to 25. Some participants who were older had had as many as 50 aspects during their lives.

In preparing a questionnaire for this research, it was necessary to know as much as possible about the nature of the Vertex in each of the 12 signs. For this, we are indebted to Delphine Jay's article, "The Third Dimension of Self: the Vertex," and to Ruth Dewey's article, "The Vertex-AntiVertex, What It Is and How to Determine It." We also looked into the hundreds of events we researched to gain additional understanding of how this axis works in real life. Some of the results follow:

Vertex in Aries or Mars in Close Aspect

You are expected to:

- Pick up the reigns of leadership.

- Initiate new directions.

- Take a decisive stand.

- Overcome inhibitions and activate personal drive.

- Learn courage and conquer fears.

Doing so may:

- Satisfy a fundamental expressional need you are psychologically ready to fulfill.

- Challenge your ability to lead, troubleshoot, or innovate.

- Bring forward from your depths abilities that you were not consciously aware of.

- Establish your awareness of the personal courage and self-identity you need.

Not doing so may:

- Put the initiative into another's hands.

- Leave you unfulfilled because you have compromised or fallen into tempting mediocrity.

- Create a personality gap through a psychologically damaging identity complex.

When the Vertex progresses into Aries or an Aries Vertex is involved in an aspect, a new start is sometimes forced on the person. He may feel ready to make a new start. This may be through some pioneering effort since one is developing the courage to take initiative and to be more self-assertive. The house with Aries on the cusp is activated. One with this could become involved in military matters, police work, or any physically active endeavor. He could discover depths of ability he never knew he had as he blazes a new trail in whatever area of interest he is involved.

One person had to "start over" after her house had burned down. Another traveled to initiate a new business in another area.

Vertex in Taurus or Venus in Close Aspect
You are expected to:

- Complete something already set in motion.

- Become self-sustaining or self-supporting.

- Deal with a security problem.

- Be called on to gain support for the arts in some way.

- Learn to deal with the world on a material level.

Doing so may:

- Create a solution for a severe lack, material or emotional, without a dependency on others.

- Enable you to deal with the world on a material level.

Not doing so may:

- Not bring you the self-esteem that you could gain from being self-sufficient.

- Bring you subtle feelings of social or emotional indebtedness.

When the Vertex progresses into Taurus or a Taurus Vertex is involved in a progression, your ability to deal with the material world is brought out. This includes not only testing your own ability to make money but also handling the changes that come from your purchasing power. Caring for your possessions is developed too, or you learn from the consequences of not caring for them. Issues involving a sense of self-worth are critical. Tonsils, the voice, vocal cords, or the throat can be areas of concern. This is a period when one might explore sensual pleasures such as the arts or anything else that appeals to the senses.

For one 11-year-old, his family built a new house, and he had his own room for the first time.

Vertex in Gemini or Mercury in Close Aspect

You are expected to:

- Bring your ability to communicate or write to the fore.

- Use hard-core facts to clarify a situation.

- Come up with ideas and present them clearly.

- Speak, write, or instruct.

- Debate your own viewpoint.

- Be elected a spokesperson.

Doing so may:

- Improve your ability to be understood by choosing your words carefully and having the facts to back them up.

- Gain the confidence to speak out since you have greater skill to make yourself understood.

- Maintain a youthful curiosity so that you will be prepared with facts when tested.

Not doing so you may:

- Generalize or go off on a tangent, losing the point you are trying to make.

- Avoid the research and mental flexibility this clarity demands.

- Get hung up on one goal instead of developing the diversity you need.

When the Vertex progresses into Gemini or a Gemini Vertex is involved in any progression, travel, learning, and educational tests were frequently mentioned. This often marks the beginning of a time when one must start to use his education and produce results with the facts he has learned. It may bring the purchase of a car and the need for much local travel or commuting. It is a period when youthful attitudes and flexibility pay off as well as the ability to communicate in all kinds of situations with well-documented facts. Issues involving siblings may arise as well.

One individual began a career in communications as a director and producer. He had much travel out of the country and received awards for excellence.

Vertex in Cancer or the Moon in Close Aspect

You are expected to:

- Deal with the public or in the public interest.

- Handle the emotional factor in situations.

- Learn to deal with women or public figures.

- Develop your ability to spot trends and accept the background parental role you must play as opposed to the foreground administrative role of the Capricorn AntiVertex.

- Discover and acknowledge the emotional side of your nature.

Doing so may:

- Help you to develop the nurturing qualities and recognize your own dependency needs as legitimate areas in your life.

- Discover a place where you play the parent role to the world.

Not doing so you may:

- Be at the mercy of emotional factors in others that distort situations for you.

- Create conflict from those who feel you have let them down.

- Give in to the temptation to suppress the emotions.

When the Vertex progresses into Cancer or a Cancer Vertex is involved in any progressed aspect, the wish is often to be at home. For many, though, there is a need to be away from the home. Some leave to go to college or travel for their businesses. Some will get into nurturing roles for their families or their careers. Patriotism, self-protectiveness, and shyness sometimes are stronger than before. Real estate transactions may be made too. Depending on a person's age, parents or one's role as a parent is important. It is an emotional time when one has to deal with emotional and family matters. The person is learning to express his feelings.

One young woman had graduated from high school and went away to college at this time. She found it very painful to separate from her parents.

Vertex in Leo or the Sun in Close Aspect

You are expected to:

- Become an individual instead of one of many.

- Project your own emotions in a special relationship instead of the easier separativeness of the emotions of the group, which the Aquarius AVx offers.

- Be responsible for teaching, working on an entertainment

project, or dealing with young people or children.

- Acknowledge and accept your need for admiration.

Doing so you may:

- Become aware of your own individuality or creative expression.

- Give outer expression to the affectional, creative side of your nature.

- Strengthen your own ego by developing it in another.

- Instill confidence and self-worth in those around you due to your magnetism and dignity.

Not doing so may:

- Lead to a psychologically crippling ego-complex.

- Bring conflict within you as you receive the same impersonal treatment you find to be the easy path of the Aquarius AVx.

When the Vertex progresses into Leo or a Leo Vertex is involved in any aspect, there is a greater need to feel like an important individual. You want your self-worth to be recognized and admired. You must do something that gives you self-esteem, pleasure or entertainment, and appreciation from others. In some cases this is a new job or attitude. Sometimes a major purchase gives this added self-esteem. If these attributes are already strong, they can be used to instill confidence and self-worth in others. There are experiences that bring out your ability to stand out from the crowd.

One nine-year-old learned to ride a bicycle even though it had only one pedal. He bartered for chocolate bubble gum. These gave him a sense of importance and accomplishment.

Vertex in Virgo or Mercury in Close Aspect

You are expected to:

- Use your practical insights.

- Use your abilities to discover flaws.

- Give mundane service.

- Compile material for practical use.

- Supply work details.

- Develop your discriminatory faculties.

- Be a useful and productive member of society.

- Develop a conscientious application and ability to accept criticism.

Doing so may:

- Make you feel useful in the world in order to offset a health complex.

- Enable you to accept your own self-worth regardless of the opinions of others.

- Enable you to function at your most efficient level knowing that your life has meaning.

Not doing so may:

- Bring inner conflict by giving in to confusion or being hard to find.

- Put yourself in a position to live with disorder and a feeling of uselessness.

When the Vertex progresses in to Virgo or a Virgo Vertex makes any aspect, you are expected to use your analytical abilities and practicality in service to humanity. You discover your ability to discriminate and see flaws others miss. You can make wonderful contributions to the health fields. Some are called on to serve in the fashion or clothing industry causing you to discover previously unknown abilities in these areas. You can bring order out of chaos with your practical ability to store and classify the many details of life. You could serve through helping yourself. Others become more diet and health-conscious.

One person had chicken pox (health) and also got a puppy (small animal).

Vertex in Libra or Venus in Close Aspect

You are expected to:

- Bring opposing factions together, counsel or arbitrate on a fair and equal basis, or seek a satisfactory compromise.

- Gain a cooperative spirit and sense of fair play to move forward.

- Become conscious of a possible persecution complex, which brings inner conflict.

- Relate equally to others in order to have inner balance from socially opposing demands.

- Cultivate the arts of compromise and detachment.

Doing so you may:

- Put aside personal ego and identify in partnerships.

- Relate to others on an equal basis with a sense of justice in these relationships.

- Accept the need for balance in the life and environment.

Not doing so you may:

- Be biased in judgment and add to the agitation.

- Make demands, which would ally you with the self-centeredness that would deepen relationship inhibitions.

- Fall into both indecisiveness and inertia.

When the Vertex progresses into Libra or a Libra Vertex makes any aspect, one becomes adept at expressing some of Libra's greatest attributes: bringing opposing factions together so they can work well. You are relating to other people; for some this means entering or leaving a marriage contract or working on changes in a marriage relationship. There is a strong need to relate to another on an equal basis. In relating with others or getting others to relate, there are many times when compromise is needed while still retaining equality in the relationship in a fair and impartial way.

One 47-year-old man not only began making changes in his own marriage when the Vertex progressed into Libra but he also helped a friend with problems in his marriage.

Vertex in Scorpio or Pluto or Mars in Close Aspect

You are expected to:

- Learn total self-mastery.

- Explore the limits of your desires and appetites, defining the limits not only in terms of self but also out of respect for the rights of others.

- Assist others in terms of mutual monies, the dead or dying, reform or healing.

- Develop interest in business practices.

- Reform or recycle what is obsolete.

- Give concrete assistance to partnership security.

- Acquaint yourself with metaphysics in order to sharpen perspective, gain a sense of collective values, and bring occult knowledge forward.

Doing so you may:

- Express an inner emotional need to reform.

- Recycle what is obsolete.

- Find personal rebirth each time you are tested from the appetites of the lower nature (Taurus AVx) to the regenerative or healing strength of the higher.

- Be reborn to the higher self.

Not doing so you may:

- Bow to base material desires of others creating a smoldering resentment in you.

- Have conflict from emotional insecurity.

When the Vertex progresses into Scorpio or a Scorpio Vertex makes any aspect, you may be dealing with life or death matters. Other's deaths or near death experiences could cause you to deal with our own mortality. Sexual issues ranging from sexual crimes to facing your own need for a sexual relationship may come up. Surgeries or the "cutting away" of something could be of concern including abortion issues-yours or another's. As you learn self-mastery you are setting up limits for yourself as you explore not only how far your desires can take you but also about your need to respect others' rights. You are learning about the rights of others too as you handle mutual finances.

A 66-year-old man's son-in-law who lived in the man's house was diagnosed with recurrent cancer. This made the man more concerned about his own mortality.

Vertex in Sagittarius or Jupiter in Close Aspect

You are expected to:

- Develop a broader vision of things.

- Develop a deeper understanding of the significance behind the facts- even behind life, like a religious consciousness or a philosophical view of things.

- Become inspired by reaching toward truth.

- Travel or attain a higher education.

- Deal with a legal principle.

- Teach a class dealing with religion or philosophy.

- Editorialize, promote, or bring understanding to a situation.

Doing so may:

- Teach you to have faith in yourself, your abilities, and your goals in life.

- Teach you that faith in self must come from faith in something outside the self.

Not doing so may:

- Incline you to accept a law or principle without looking past the facts to see how it will actually affect people.

- Find it difficult to accept the accolades and rewards you have earned and, instead, drift aimlessly through life.

When the Vertex progresses into Sagittarius or a Sagittarius Vertex makes any aspect, one's life is to expand in understanding of religious or philosophical principles or of life itself. This can come through metaphysical or religious principles or an event, which gives you the freedom to be yourself or to open up. Sometimes foreign travel broadens your understanding. You may have to deal with the principles of things such as laws, policies, or rules. You may teach or write about what you've learned and, in doing so, gain faith in your own abilities. Sports or outdoor experiences could be the vehicle for attaining expanded insights.

One woman said that her mother had died just before the sign change. She then felt a newness and freedom to "be me" opening up.

Vertex in Capricorn or Saturn in Close Aspect
You are expected to:

- Accept the fact that duties and obligations carried out prepare you for positions of greater responsibility.

- Accept limitations and diligently work through them.

- Realize that you are being forced to develop organizational ability, caution, prudence, and patience.

- Possibly run for an office at a time when no one else wants it.

- Accept limitations whether they are self-imposed or imposed by the outside world.

Doing so may:

- Make you aware of how much your organizing ability is needed.

- Purify the self through struggle and restriction.

- **Not doing so may:**

- Keep you from moving up in position and prestige as a result of your undependability, instability, or current excuses such as claiming a lack of time due to domestic considerations.

- Have inner conflict from becoming the victim of an unstable environment (Cancer AVx).

- Cause subtle inferiority feelings from your lack of discipline.

When the Vertex progresses into Capricorn or a Capricorn Vertex makes any aspect, career promotions and job offers may figure prominently. Concern for one's image becomes more important in such ways as losing weight, changing drinking patterns, or changing boy or girl friends if dating one who is inappropriate. For a child, one might fit in better or want to fit in better with the mainstream. Now one begins to learn the lessons of organization, structure, and conformity. If there are struggles and restrictions, one is being challenged to grow stronger and more patient. These duties and obligations prepare the person to discover his ability for the administrative roles he will be capable of handling.

One woman said she felt her life was not going anywhere, so she quit drinking and lost weight. Then she broke up with a long-time lover.

Vertex in Aquarius or Uranus or Saturn in Close Aspect

You are expected to:

- Deal with all kinds of people, even those you feel you cannot tolerate.

- Develop enough detachment to rise above individual pettiness.

- ee no strangers, only "brothers."

- Grow through developing true individuality, unfettered by peer group pressures.

- Accept the idea that you are one among equals.

Doing so may:

- Help you avoid feelings of superiority (Leo AVx) or being too important to bother being a friend.

- Help you overcome your own ego.

- **Not doing so may:**

- Find you the object of intolerance from any group you are prejudiced against.

- Cause you to be blocked by those you are against since they are unable to create the future openings you need.

- Make accomplishments become as nothing and the impact you hope to make on the world fall short of your expectations.

When the Vertex progresses into Aquarius or an Aquarius Vertex makes any aspect, you may rebel against previous conditions. The urge to be one's own person is strong. Independence becomes increasingly important. As you become more of an individual, you learn to accept the individuality and uniqueness of others. Barriers against the ideals of brotherhood are being broken down during this period. You may be the object of intolerance from others if you do not learn tolerance toward diverse kinds of people. It is your own ego that must be overcome by dropping your sense of superiority.

One woman was increasingly unhappy with the restrictions from her husband. Another wanted to dress in her own style- "even if I'm not in sync with everyone else.

Vertex in Pisces or Jupiter or Neptune in Close Aspect

You are expected to:

- Develop selflessness and emotional or psychological insights rather than the practical, material insights of the Virgo AVx.

- Develop compassion and the ability to listen to another who may be hurting inside and simply need to know someone cares.

- Be of service in areas of confinement, institutions, or places where work must be done quietly behind the scenes.

- Accept the fact that you are children of the universe and are here in order to convey the ideal of infinite love and beauty to your less aware brethren.

Doing so you may:

- Grow through those you have assisted or because of the insights you have beyond practical considerations.

- Realize that you are basically secure in your knowledge of the scheme of things.

Not doing so you may:

• Turn back into yourself for the discovery of things you already know.

• Have a sense of futility, which can lead to despair and the resulting self-destruction.

When the Vertex progresses into Pisces or when a Pisces Vertex makes any aspect, Neptune issues come to the fore: allergies, lack of structure, idealizations, lack of reality, inspiration, or looking for perfection or God. The urge for escape and deception may manifest. Through it all, one develops greater compassion for others. Use the psychological insights gained through this period by listening to others. Service given quietly through institutions or in private can bring out your ability to give infinite love and beauty to those who are less aware. Your growth comes from expressing emotional and psychological insights rather than material ones.

One started his second year of college. He felt he had a lack of structure, and was figuring out what he wanted to do. Another started playing football, which he idolized.

Combining the Ascendant, Midheaven and Vertex

As Delphine Jay says, the Vertex symbolizes what is expected of us as a result of what we are (Ascendant) and what we do (Midheaven). To illustrate, because a person with a Virgo Ascendant is meticulous and analytical, he may pursue a career or be known for his factual knowledge and ability to communicate (Gemini Midheaven). As a result, the world expects him to independently express his uniqueness (Vertex in Aquarius) and to tolerate all kinds of people.

The quality represented by the sign of the Vertex is being pulled out of you. It is needed for your personality completion. A person with a Sagittarius Ascendant, because he is expansive, cheerful, and philosophical, who deals with the analysis of details (Virgo MC), is learning to express emotions and family matters to round out his personality. This person may be tempted to go toward his Capricorn AntiVertex and deal with administrative matters because it is comfortable, but this will not enable him to develop what he needs, the Cancer qualities of his Cancer Vertex.

Another example is having the charm and beauty of a Libra Ascendant and doing the emotional, nurturing family things represented by a Cancer MC, a person could be expected to deal with the money matters, artistic expression, values or self-worth of the Taurus Vertex to complete her personality. One who had this combination was Diana, Princess of Wales.

One with a Cancer Ascendant is a nurturing person who can express his feelings and emotions, so he is in a position to serve humanity through philanthropy, expressing compassion, or seeking perfection through his Pisces MC. As a result the world expects him to develop a deeper understanding of the significance of facts, a religious consciousness, or deal with legal principles expected of his Sagittarius Vertex. He has to have faith in himself and his abilities. One with this combination is Bill Gates of Microsoft.

The combinations (Ascendant/Midheaven/Vertex) of some well-known people are listed below.

Vertex in Aries

Libra/Cancer/Aries	Woodrow Wilson
Libra/Cancer/Aries	Bill Clinton
Libra/Cancer/Aries	Cecil Rhodes
Libra/Cancer/Aries	Barbara Walters

Libra/Cancer/Aries	Elizabeth Taylor

Vertex in Taurus

Libra/Cancer/Taurus	Harry Truman
Libra/Cancer/Taurus	Monica Lewinsky
Libra/Cancer/Taurus	Bill Bradley
Libra/Cancer/Taurus	Jeffrey Dahmer
Libra/Cancer/Taurus	John F. Kennedy

Vertex in Gemini

Scorpio/Leo/Gemini	Whoopi Goldburg
Libra/Cancer/Gemini	David Koresh
Libra/Cancer/Gemini	Jimmy Carter
Scorpio/Leo/Gemini	Bertrand Russell
Scorpio/Leo/Gemini	Ann Baxter

Vertex in Cancer

Scorpio/Leo/Cancer	Gandhi
Scorpio/Leo/Gemini	Clint Eastwood
Sagittarius/Libra/Cancer	Eleanor Roosevelt
Sagittarius/Libra/Cancer	Fred Astaire
Scorpio/Leo/Cancer	Jackie Kennedy Onassis

Vertex in Leo

Capricorn/Scorpio/Leo	Jesse Jackson
Sagittarius/Scorpio/Leo	Prince William
Sagittarius/Libra/Leo	Mother Teresa
Scorpio/Leo/Leo	Fidel Castro

Capricorn/Libra/Leo   Candice Bergen

Vertex in Virgo
Aquarius/Sagittarius/Virgo   Catherine the Great
Capricorn/Scorpio/Virgo   Queen Elizabeth II
Aquarius/Sagittarius/Virgo   Audry Hepburn
Aquarius/Sagittarius/Virgo   Mary Martin
Pisces/Sagittarius/Virgo   Robert Redford

Vertex in Libra
Aries/Capricorn/Libra   Bill Cosby
Gemini/Aquarius/Libra   Samuel Hahnemann
Taurus/Capricorn/Libra   Martin Luther King
Aries/Capricorn/Libra   Barbra Streisand
Taurus/Aqurius/Libra   Vivian Leigh

Vertex in Scorpio
Gemini/Aquarius/Scorpio   Henry Kissinger
Cancer/Pisces/Scorpio   Saddam Hussein
Gemini/Pisces/Scorpio   Teddy Roosevelt
Aries/Capricorn/Scorpio   Helen Reddy
Cancer/Pisces/Scorpio   Judy Garland

Vertex in Sagittarius
Leo/Aries/Sagittarius   Thomas Jefferson
Aries/Cancer/Sagittarius   Marilyn Monroe
Leo/Aries/Sagittarius   Meryl Streep
Leo/Aries/Sagittarius   Prince Charles

Leo/Aries/Sagittarius   Naomi Judd

Vertex in Capricorn
Leo/Taurus/Capricorn   Christopher Reeves
Leo/Taurus/Capricorn   O. J. Simpson
Leo/Taurus/Capricorn   Donald Trump
Leo/Aries/Capricorn   Prince Andrew
Leo/Taurus/Capricorn   Vanessa Redgrave

Vertex in Aquarius
Virgo/Gemini/Aquarius   John F. Kennedy, Jr.
Virgo/Gemini/Aquarius   George Bush, Sr.
Cancer/Aries/Aquarius   Ivy Goldstein-Jacobson
Virgo/Gemini/Aquarius   Louisa May Alcott
Virgo/Gemini/Aquarius   Richard Nixon

Vertex in Pisces
Virgo/Gemini/Pisces   Franklin D. Roosevelt
Virgo/Gemini/Pisces   Winston Churchill
Virgo/Gemini/Pisces   Emily Dickenson
Virgo/Gemini/Pisces   Doris Day
Virgo/Gemini/Pisces   Julie Andrews

4

Aspects of the Vertex

Before buying my computer I believed that the only Vertex aspects that seemed to "work" were the conjunctions and the oppositions. These still seem to provide the most vivid results, but with the computer I could work with many years, a project much too time consuming when these angles are calculated by hand. So, for some charts, I run the Vertex progressions from and to natal planets and angles for the entire lifetime. It was only then that I began to see results from sextiles, squares, trines, and quincunxes. I suspect that the semi-square and sesquisquare give results too.

The research we've done does not show a clear theme or meaning for the Vertex beyond the idea of its being what the world expects of a person as a result of who he is and what he does and the other ideas already discussed. The most reliable interpretation is that it is an **activator** or **catalyst** of the action or conditions described by the planet or position being activated. It does seem that we have little or no control of the events of the Vertex, and, in that sense, events are fated.

In every case it is necessary to consider:

• The sign of the Vertex

- The house of the Vertex

- The nature of the aspect

- The sign and nature of the planet or sensitive point

- The house of the planet or sensitive point

- The natural rulership of the planet

- The house(s) ruled by the planet

- The aspects to the Vertex

- The aspects to the planet

We researched only the 10 planets (eight planets plus the Sun and Moon), the other two angles (Ascendant and Midheaven), progressed Vertex aspects to the natal Vertex, and the ingresses of signs and houses by secondary progression. Only the five Ptolemaic aspects and the quincunx were used. I have recently done some work with the declinations too. This is not to say that other factors are not significant, but a study must be clearly limited. It is hoped that others will broaden this research to include other factors.

We did not find that sextiles and trines are always favorable, but they usually were. When they were not favorable, the person usually handled them well or had resources for doing so. Nor were squares, oppositions, and quincunxes always unfavorable, but they usually were. As with any of these three aspects, the person often has the opportunity for greater development or he faces difficult events or conditions. His greatest growth comes at these times. It must be remembered that when isolating a factor (the Vertex) that other aspects may also be in effect. The nature of the planet involved determines the outcome too.

The conjunctions were most often in the nature of the planet.

These (and the parallels) were the strongest of the aspects. Quincunxes were also mixed although most required changes and adjustments for the person.

Conjunctions

Conjunctions (and parallels) are the most powerful aspects of all. The outcome of events shown by Vertex conjunctions depends heavily on the planet or angle involved. A lack of perspective is associated with this aspect (unlike the opposition, which indicates awareness). One is often so wrapped up in his own needs and desires that he is oblivious to others. With the Vertex involved, though, he must confront and deal with others since the Vertex is on the western side of the chart.

The number of responses we got in our research project is given. CR = can't remember or no answer given.

p Vx conjunct n Sun   2 responses, 0 CR

p Sun conjunct n Vx   3 responses, 1 CR

These often pertain to **self-esteem issues, children, pride or relationships**. A male figure is sometimes involved. **Promotions or career changes** are possible, or one experiences change in his feelings of importance. **Recuperation** from illnesses is good.

A 40-year-old woman had several important events at the time of this progression. She began dating her future husband (Sun) as this aspect began to be within one degree of the conjunction. They married one or two months after the aspect was exact. The Sun is natally in the fifth of romance and children. A stepson moved into their home, and there were some problems with the stepson's adjustment to their marriage. A third important event was that she made a career change. She changed from physical medicine and rehab to pediatrics (Sun—chil-

dren). Natally, the Vertex is in her sixth of work in Libra (marriage).

p Vx conjunct n Moon	9 responses, 1 CR
p Moon conjunct n Moon	7 responses, 1 CR

These were often emotional or **family** events. Many, but not all, were events pertaining to a **woman** in their lives. Some involved changes in their **home**, such as having people entering or leaving their home, and a few were **health** issues.

In one case a woman, who has her Vertex and Moon both in the 6th of work and health matters, had a very emotional scene with an older woman, a chiropractor, who was her mentor. The older woman was not only helping her with her studies for a career in medical fields but also providing her with a home. The clash was partly due to the older woman's alcoholism (Sun semisquare Neptune). The student moved out.

p Mercury conjunct n Vx	2 responses, 0 CR
p Vx conjunct n Mercury	4 responses, 0 CR

Mercury conjunctions could pertain to **work, employees, contracts, study,** or **communications**. One could gain or lose a job or have difficulty with a **co-worker**. Contacts with **agents, writing, siblings, pets** (small animals), and **automobiles** are possible too.

A 36-year-old woman got a cat when this aspect occurred (Mercury—natural ruler of the sixth). She also bought a home after going back and forth for several months with her real estate agent over the contract for it. Another person lost his job, and a third person experienced the death of his brother (Mercury).

p Venus conjunct n Vx	6 responses, 0 CR

p Vx conjunct n Venus   3 responses, 0 CR

Venus conjunctions involve strong **relationships** or at least a pleasant and **happy period** in one's life. They stimulate **love** and **sexual attraction** as well as a **love of beautiful things**. Social affairs flourish. Healthwise, there may be concerns with the **throat, kidneys, blood clots**, or **veins**. Venus also rules **young women**.

While these aspects brought romance and marriage to some, one young man had a very powerful nurturing, protective relationship with a young woman even though it was "on again, off again." Another had a pleasant time when she got into gourmet cooking and caring for plants. Yet a third person had breast cancer, a lumpectomy, and radiation treatments. Ivy Goldstein-Jacobson had this conjunction in her ninth house at the time of her death. Venus rules her fourth—the end of life.

p Mars conjunct n Vx   4 responses, 0 CR

p Vx conjunct n Mars   6 responses, 0 CR

Mars' conjunctions with the Vertex can indicate work with **machinery, strife, anger, jealousy, aggressive action**, and **contacts with young men**. Whether these are favorable or not depends on the aspects and the signs. **Military** and **police service** is possible too. For women, it often indicates an **important male figure** in their life. For a child, there could be strife with a stepfather.

A 13-year-old girl with a Sagittarius Ascendant asserted her independence by enrolling in a college preparatory course without family approval. She did well and later received a scholarship for a university. She had the same aspect again at age 50 when she had a renewed interest in the concerts and activities of a British rock band with four male members. She wrote an astrological profile of the lead singer, and this interest led to interesting and warm connections and friendships.

Princess Diana had this at the time of her accident, which resulted in her death. It was in the eighth house and only three minutes past the exact.

p Vx conjunct n Jupiter 5 responses, 0 CR

This aspect of **luck** and **protection** also brings **a desire for wealth** and personal **comfort**. It represents **justice** and **fair play** and opportunities for **gains in knowledge**. People **of different races** or backgrounds can enter your life. **Educated people** and people who have wealth may influence you too. You may have contact with **people in foreign countries**.

One man got a new position as a result of an inheritance when his father-in-law died which resulted in acquiring many new friends. This gave him greater affluence.

p Vx conjunct n Saturn 8 responses, 0 CR

p Saturn conjunct n Vx 1 response, 0 CR

This brings **hardships, delays** and **inhibitions**. It usually maps a **difficult** time according to the house(s) Saturn tenants and rules. If it is the seventh, divorce or difficulties in the marriage. If the fifth, **trouble with one's children** or **lovers**. There can be heavy **responsibilities**. People who enter the life under this are apt to be **older people** or very serious, matured individuals. One may develop patience and discipline, however.

One teenaged girl lost self-esteem after losing out on being a cheerleader. Another person with the Vx in the sixth (health) began working in oncology in a children's medical center. Children dying of cancer became increasingly emotionally difficult for her, so she soon changed. Her Vertex is trine Jupiter (she was able to change) square Pluto (death and dying).

p Vx conjunct n Uranus   6 responses, 2 CR

One may **rebel** against **rules, regulations** and **authority figures** under this. Some will selfishly demand personal **freedom** and **independence** whether ready for it or not. Others may find old **conditions breaking up unexpectedly** as one breaks out of a rut. This break-up may seem devastating, yet as we look back at the event years later, we see it was good for our own growth.

One woman met her future husband at the time of this progression through friends (Uranus). She described friendship as the best thing about her relationship.

p Vx conjunct n Neptune   5 responses, 0 CR

Negatively, this can bring **confusion, deception, sorrow** or **self-analysis. Drug** and **alcohol** problems can manifest. If used positively, it enhances one's **sensitivity, artistic interests, dancing** and **spiritual development**. One may be involved with anything that creates an **illusion**: films, photography, cosmetology, make-up, or special effects.

One woman said that a friend was having an affair with her husband. Another individual endured favoritism at the office. A teenager used this energy more constructively in band activities in his high school.

p Vx conjunct n Pluto   7 responses, 0 CR

Often something is **discarded** or **taken away** from the life to make way for the new. There are **transformations** and **drastic changes**. The most drastic of all is being influenced by someone's **death**. Sometimes there is concern about matters of **inheritances, taxes,** and support (or its lack) from others. Some people take out **loans** under this.

One 15-year-old girl's mother died. Her Vertex is in the eighth. She was adjusting to living with her father without the mother. It was difficult and awkward for both. Her father was upset when she came home late from the prom, and she was devastated at his lack of trust.

p Vx conjunct n Ascendant
    Does not occur in northern latitudes

p Vx conjunct n Midheaven   4 responses, 0 CR

Although neither of these is an energy, it does seem to produce events. We get the meaning from the Midheaven, which pertains to a **parent** or the **career**, in other words, **what a person does**. A job or **career change** or events pertaining to a parent may occur.

One woman who had this went to work as usual on a Monday only to discover that her father (Midheaven) had sold the business that she worked for. She retained her job, but she was no longer the boss's daughter. Other events were that one woman was elected to an office in a national society, one lost her mother, and one was getting used to fatherhood.

Sextiles

Sextiles are mentally energizing. One is so eager for new experiences that he attracts opportunities. Only if he acts on these opportunities, though, will he reap the benefits. Negative events that occur with these Vertex sextiles almost always have a side or result that is somehow beneficial. There is danger of scattering the energies too much and thereby losing some of the opportunities they represent. If one's enthusiasms are sustained, though, sextiles can indicate some brilliance or sparks of creativity.

p Vx sextile n Sun   10 responses, 2 CR

p Sun sextile n Vx   16 responses, 4 CR

This sextile can bring opportunities for a **gain in status**, usually through a **male figure**. There may be **promotions** or some **recognition** for your work. **Creative efforts** can succeed, and one could have the chance to participate in sports events. This can be an asset if a person is trying for some **leadership** position.

One woman got a promotion at work. She felt that her superiors (Sun) were supporting her efforts (Vx in the eighth). Before the aspect had waned, her husband had a successful serious surgery.

p Vx sextile n Moon   13 responses, 4 CR

p Moon sextile n Vx   11 responses, 1 CR

These usually involve **women, moves, emotional events,** or **domestic arrangements.** A person could get a job in a restaurant. Others may have the opportunity to work out problems in their marriages. The time may be right for **buying a new home**, or the **sale of a home** could go well.

One woman bought a new home in a new city. The work she and her husband did required much travel (progressed Vertex in the ninth) and she was able to take her son along when they traveled. She also began to show Great Dane dogs (Moon in Virgo).

p Vx sextile n Mercury   13 responses, 1 CR

p Mercury sextile n Vx   23 responses, 2 CR

One could **start school**. This would be elementary school or kindergarten for a child or college for an adult. At the very least a person may have **new mental interests** and become more **mentally active** than before. Mercury rules **neighborhoods** and **siblings** as well. Some may **write** or **travel** more. Some may find ways to work out problems through **communication**.

For one 11-year-old the neighborhood kids were bullying her. They had been friends until the bullying started. A teacher forced them to be together until they worked out their problems. They did, and she no longer felt trapped in her own home.

p Vx sextile n Venus	13 responses, 4 CR
p Venus sextile n Vx	9 responses, 1 CR

Expect **love** and **romance** to work out well when this is in effect. With other indications too, it can indicate the happy events associated with a **marriage**, your own or someone else's. You have the opportunity to **work out marriage problems** or **problems with a female boss** or co-worker. **Social events** and the purchase of **luxury items** are favored. Changes made in one's life are usually happy ones.

The sister of a woman with her Vertex in Gemini married, and this same woman cut her arm badly (Gemini) on a glass door. For another person, her female boss left, much to her relief. Her Vertex is in the sizth house.

p Vx sextile n Mars	15 responses, 1 CR
p Mars sextile n Vx	7 responses, 5 CR

Events include being **active in sports** or **meeting a future husband** or some male figure who is important to you. One person began therapy with a **male** counselor. It maps an active time when one may **start an exercise program** or have an urge to do **heavy gardening**. Your **energy** should be **high**, and **health** and **vitality** tend to be excellent.

One woman with her natal Vertex in Gemini in the eighth square

Mars had a serious car accident when this sextile occurred. She was on crutches and had physical therapy for some time after this, but she did recover completely.

p Vx sextile n Jupiter   15 responses, 1 CR

You may **travel** or have **contact with foreign countries** or people from foreign countries. **Education** is favored and some enter college or graduate school. You may be **writing** for the school paper or for publication, or **expanding** your horizons through **volunteer work**. Young people may expand their lives by getting their own apartment or home. Significant **religious events** may occur, such as having one's first communion.

One 25-year-old male graduated from graduate school and interviewed for a job, which he got (Jupiter—higher education). His natal Vertex in Pisces is in the sixth of work, making trines to Saturn, Venus, and the Sun in the second, so these events brought opportunities (sextile) to increase income (second house).

p Vx sextile n Saturn   9 responses, 1 CR

These events bring a **willingness to accept responsibilities, delays**, and **discipline**. The **laborious effort** one puts into accomplishing his goals **pays off.** Sometimes a person has to go to **work** to help meet family expenses. Sometimes there are **illnesses** in the family and the person willingly helps care for this person.

One 6-year-old female had a serious illness, which prevented her from starting school the year her friends did, so she felt lonely. She liked reading books and developed a self-reliance others didn't have.

p Vx sextile n Uranus   13 responses, 2 CR

If a person has felt that she did not have as much **personal freedom** as she wanted and needed, this aspect can make it easier for her to gain this freedom. You want to develop your **individuality**. **Friends** are beneficial in helping one do this. Events happen **suddenly**, although you might have had them in the back of your mind for some time, and now seems like the time to act making them seem sudden to others. You can make great strides in learning to use **computers** or in learning **astrology**.

A 22-year-old woman began her first professional job on a newspaper using computers and other technology. She also began living alone for the first time in her life, allowing her greater freedom and individuality. (Her Vertex is sextile planets in the ninth and tenth. Uranus is in her sixth of work).

p Vx sextile n Neptune   16 responses, 3 CR

Someone's **drinking, drugs, confusion**, a **lack of reality**, and escape often influenced these events. Some, though, pertained to **beauty, the arts, swimming** and **daydreaming**. One was teaching in a Catholic school next to a convent (Neptune). It is usually a time to pursue **spiritual goals** more than material ones. Beginning work in the **medical** fields or any kind of **service** that involves caring for others is favored too. Problems that come from being too **naïve** can be overcome.

A ten-year-old began swimming. She entered competitions in California and Hawaii. A 40-year-old woman was hired to work in a Catholic school before her degree was granted so there was some confusion about her status.

p Vx sextile n Pluto   10 responses, 1 CR

Drastic changes, deaths, surgeries, and **power struggles** are the subjects of events that occur under this aspect. The **dark side** of life often comes to the fore, but, being a sextile, a person has a better chance of handling it constructively than otherwise. **Rebirth** and **regeneration** can occur when one purges and removes what is no longer useful in his life. Emotions are deep and **intense**, and **loyalty is strong**.

A 33-year-old woman was getting bad checks from her employer. She had worked for him for six years. The employer's finances were in chaos. She quit the job, opening herself up to the prospect of getting a more reliable employer. Her Vertex is in Taurus in the eighth (money).

p Vx sextile n Ascendant
    Does not occur in northern latitudes.

p Vx sextile n Midheaven   22 responses, 4 CR

p Midheaven sextile n Vx   13 responses, 4 CR

There are opportunities for changes in one's **reputation, work** or **career**, and honors. One's **parents** may reap the benefits from something they've done in their lives. A **move** you have been wanting may also occur because when the Midheaven is activated, the fourth house cusp is too. Also, this can **enhance other aspects** that are in effect at the same time.

A 23-year-old man had great anxiety about possibly having to go to Viet Nam. Fortunately, he just missed the draft. His son had a seizure due to a high fever, but there were no seizures after that. His Vertex is in Leo (children).

P Vx sextile n Vx   11 responses, 2 CR

The **opportunity** to do something that the person had wanted for some time was present. These were **enjoyable events** or beneficial in some way. Some had long-lasting effects.

One put in a bookstore, which she had wanted to do for many years. Another person had a job on an oil rig. He worked ten hours a day working very hard, but the money he gained was certainly beneficial.

A third person had wedding showers, marriage, and a honeymoon in the Caribbean. A fourth person retired and spent two months in Norway.

Squares

While the square is usually the most difficult aspect to deal with, its cardinal quality does provide us with the concentrated energy to bring about our greatest development.

Squares challenge us to act rather than continue to endure pain. We are motivated to confront conflicting forces that can only be resolved by these encounters. With Vertex squares it is often others who prod us into this kind of development.

p Vx square n Sun	16 responses, 1 CR
p Sun square n Vx	14 responses, 2 CR

The Vertex square the Sun can bring **difficulties of the parents**, the **boss** or other **authority figures**. Parents may be on the brink of **divorce**, a parent may be ill, or the boss **terminates your employment**. Activities started at this time meet **difficulties** and **obstacles**. Your **health** may not be the best, or health matters need some attention. You need activities to build or rebuild your self-esteem.

One 16-year-old said that his father left for the last time and his parents soon divorced. He also bought his first car, became quite proficient on the violin, and had his first girlfriend, all activities that helped his self-esteem.

p Vx square n Moon	18 responses, 1 CR
p Moon square n Vx	9 responses, 0 CR

Emotional events including **death** may occur. A **parent**, particularly the mother, may **be having difficulties**. **Health** problems may occur, especially for females. Some feel tied down by **domestic duties**. Some find themselves in the role of the **caregiver** for ill relatives or friends, or they have problems with some **female**. Others find **their home unsettled** and find that they need to have frequent moves.

A girl had been very close to a neighbor woman and her son. They were like a second family to her. The neighbors moved to the other side of town. To the girl, it felt like the loss of her support system.

p Vx square n Mercury	19 responses, 0 CR
p Mercury square n Vx	15 responses, 0 CR

Challenges come from **difficulties in communication**. This could be from needing **glasses**, or, for older people, needing a hearing aid. **Respiratory problems** are common, from simple colds or allergies, to emphysema. There can be **difficulties in learning** or with travel. Sometimes you **misunderstand** others, or they misunderstand you. Your **brothers or sisters** may be having **difficulties** too or you may get a new sibling.

When one person was two, she got a dislocated right shoulder and crushed right thumb from an accident. Her right arm was immobilized for six weeks. She learned to use her left hand and arm, and she is still ambidextrous in many ways.

p Vx square n Venus	11 responses, 3 CR
p Venus square n Vx	12 responses, 2 CR

One could be having **financial difficulties** or their **love life** is not running smoothly. Physically, concerns about the **throat, tonsils** or **veins** may manifest. Some experience the **loss of a loved**

one. Others may find that they prefer to be **lazier** than usual, neglecting many everyday chores.

One woman literally tried to murder her drunken husband. She put a plastic bag over his head, but, fortunately, the dog tore the plastic allowing him to live. Her Vertex is in the eighth and is the apex of a T-square. Venus rules her first and eighth houses.

p Vx square n Mars   18 responses, 0 CR

p Mars square n Vx   9 responses, 2 CR

The negative side of Mars energy manifests when the square manifests. There is much **anger** and **strife. Surgery, financial difficulties, too much work** and **stress from peers** are some of the possibilities. Many times a person feels **helpless** to do anything about the anger she feels and **may take** this pent-up anger **out on someone else.**

A 16-year-old unmarried woman had a baby girl. She says, "Everyone was angry with me." She didn't consider the birth to be an unfavorable event. Instead, she thought people's reactions to it were. Mars is in her fifth house of children.

p Vx square n Jupiter   16 responses, 0 CR

This aspect is **not always negative** although many times it indicates **"too much of a good thing." Study** and travel figured prominently. Sometimes there are **unsettling moves** that do not seem to solve the problems the person was moving away from. **Legal problems** are possible or difficulties with one's **in-laws. Foreigners** or **foreign places** could present problems that need to be worked out. The difficulty could come from not understanding other cultures.

One person felt he had unjustly been passed over for an honor. One

6-year-old lost his father and had to try to make sense of death at an early age. This square was present at the time the Titanic sank.

p Vx square n Saturn	10 responses, 0 CR
p Saturn square n Vx	2 responses, 1 CR

There are **no free rides** with this aspect. Confrontations with **authority** or with **males** in general occur. One may have to accept **responsibilities** he is not willing to assume. One's own **negative attitude** attracts difficulties. **Trips** taken at this time are usually taken for **business. Jobs can be lost** or be difficult in other ways. Some succumb to **depression.** With a constructive attitude one can come out of this period with a greater **maturity** and **sense of reality.**

One woman had a lover who admitted that he was married when this aspect occurred dashing her hopes for marriage. Even the birth of a son felt like a restriction to another woman due to the responsibility and lack of freedom she did not want to assume. A 13-year-old boy had trouble with algebra. Since he had not had trouble with math before, he felt that the teacher could not teach well.

p Vx square n Uranus	20 responses, 0 CR

A person with this aspect may have a strong **desire for personal freedom.** People seem to attract **unexpected events** that come up suddenly, making this a very **unstable period. Accidents, surgery, break-ups of relationships, divorce** and **sudden moves** give one the feeling that her life is out of control. Many times the changes that come under Uranus are ultimately beneficial, but they usually don't seem so at the time.

A man with this had three months of army maneuvers when it rained almost every day. He described this experience as "pure hell." Another, who was a minister's son, became aware of inherent injus-

tices in social and church bureaucracies. Uranus ruled his fourth (a parent) and tenanted his eleventh (groups and organizations).

p Vx square n Neptune   16 responses, 0 CR

Others can **easily sway** a person when this square is in effect. Sometimes **social forces** seem to be dragging a person into actions they normally would resist. **Deception, drugs, lies** and **alcohol** are too easily attracted to become a part of one's life. **Jealousies** and **secret enemies** may undermine what you are doing. You can also **deceive yourself** by seeing only what you want to see.

One woman's husband was having an affair. Another woman was hospitalized (Neptune—natural ruler of hospitals) for a hysterectomy. For another woman, there was much arguing with her husband over his alcohol consumption and their son's drug addiction. That and financial deception almost ended her marriage.

p Vx square n Pluto   16 responses, 1 CR

Drastic changes come with this aspect. The most drastic of all is **death**. One was death of a **father**. Another father committed suicide, a woman had a **miscarriage**, and a fourth **person thought her mother was dying** when the mother had a miscarriage. Power **struggles** are common. Some felt **pressured** to make changes in their lives they did not want to make. Problems with **insurance** companies or **tax** people may occur.

One 19-year-old had power struggles with her parents. Her parents saw her anti-war attitudes and independence as rebellion against them. She also changed her college major-from fashion art, which she discovered she hated, to business advertising. Her Pluto is in the fourth (parents) and the Vertex is in the sixth of work.

p Vx square n Ascendant   4 responses, 0 CR

p Ascendant square n Vx   5 responses, 1 CR

This can be a **difficult** time, which often indicates **grief** and **obstacles**. **Responsibilities** are heavy but must be met. Events can bring **chronic fatigue** and a **strain on health**.

A typical example is that of a 49-year-old woman with her Vertex in Scorpio whose husband had a heart attack and surgery. It was necessary for her to go back to work. Her mother also moved in with her and died while this aspect was still in effect.

p Vx square n Midheaven   27 responses, 3 CR

p Midheaven square n Vx   20 responses, 1 CR

This is a **challenging aspect,** which works out through a **parent,** one's **reputation** or **career**. Difficulties have to be met, and **growth** and **strength** come from finding solutions. With the Vertex involved, one has **little or no** control over the situation.

A 12-year-old child's mother (Midheaven) was to have a baby by Cesarean, but there was too much saddleblock administered, which paralyzed the mother's lungs (Gemini on the cusp of the eighth from the tenth—possible death of the mother). It was difficult to revive her, but she had the baby naturally a few days later after a difficult birth. Forceps had to be used. Mother and baby were severely jaundiced and their blood had to be cleansed.

p Vx square n Vx   8 responses, 3 CR

These mapped **difficult times** when **events beyond the person's control** brought changes.

One man lost his job when a huge defense contract for the plant he worked in was cancelled and closed down. For another man, his wife left for a foreign country, and this precipitated his divorce.

Trines

The energy of the trine is essentially creative, warming, and positive. Some say they are the rewards of our spiritual development from other lifetimes since we have built our positive use into our nature. Good luck, ease, comfort, and prosperity are easier to obtain while they are in effect than when they're not.

Often we passively receive the beneficial conditions trines represent. Unless some hard aspects are present too, though, we are inclined to be rather inactive or downright lazy because we are so content with things as they are. Vertex trines are no exception. The events that occur or the conditions we encounter tend to be pleasant and beneficial.

p Vx trine n Sun	17 responses, 1 CR
p Sun trine n Vx	13 responses, 3 CR

You get the feeling that **everything seems to succeed** easily. Your **self-esteem** is boosted. **Responsibilities ease. Changes** turn out to be beneficial even if they are not welcome changes at the time. **Happy events** may occur within the family, such as the birth of a son or brother. One woman felt very positive about her life.

A 15-year-old girl was sent to live in a small town with several relatives due to a kidnapping threat made against her. It was made because her father had testified against some well-known criminals who had robbed their store. There was a gun battle. She described the move as beneficial because she developed more self-confidence and was part of a close-knit, large family.

p Vx trine n Moon	12 responses, 2 CR
p Moon trine n Vx	7 responses, 0 CR

Family matters become more harmonious and **people feel closer** to each other. Some **move, buy new homes** or **improve their present homes.** Emotionally, it often maps a highlight of a person's life. A person may have great **rapport with the public.** For business people, a sense of **what the public wants** is heightened.

One teen regained her self-confidence by playing softball and basketball and becoming a cheerleader. She said it was one of her best years. She also made the best grades in her class. Her Vertex is in Gemini trine the Moon in the fourth.

p Vx trine n Mercury	7 responses, 0 CR

p Mercury trine n Vx	25 responses, 2 CR

This is excellent for any type of **Mercury business** or **activity, writing, lecturing, TV** or **printing.** One can **gain from printed material** such as documents, letters, books, or the Internet. **Good judgment** and **salesmanship** are highlighted, and students benefit from **the clarity of thinking** this brings. The **ability to talk** and **exchange ideas** is strong. Some find solutions for getting **respiratory allergies** under control.

One child had had very limited communication with other people due to an illness. At the time of this aspect, she was allowed increased activity and communication, which was a drastic change for her. Her Vertex is in Gemini in the eighth trine Mercury and Jupiter in the twelfth.

p Vx trine Venus	15 responses, 2 CR

p Venus trine n Vx	22 responses, 2 CR

This may be a busy period of **social functions, weddings, engagements** and **parties.** Some have salary increases, or at least fi-

nances are good. Many try to make the most of their appearance by **dressing more stylishly,** trying to **lose weight** or getting a **new hairstyle.** Some receive **gifts** of jewelry or other luxury items.

One had a crush on a boy in school. He never knew it. A 61-year-old woman said that her relationship with her husband improved greatly due to spending more time together, and their finances improved with this aspect.

p Vx trine n Mars	12 responses, 4 CR
p Mars trine n Vx	3 responses, 0 CR

You may have a **dynamic energy** level. **Ambition** is stimulated, and you have the energy to carry out your plans. **Judgment** is usually sound, but you **may have to be aggressive** in a positive sense, in order to get what you want. A **male** will figure in your activities. For women, this can be a man who will be quite important in your life.

One 32-year-old woman won a prize working crossword puzzles one month after the date of this aspect was exact. The money went to pay hospital expenses when her sixth baby was born prematurely. Expenses would have been more than she and her husband could afford. (Natal Vertex is in her eighth—jointly held money—and natal Mars is in her third—her sixth child.)

p Vx trine n Jupiter	20 responses, 2 CR
p Jupiter trine n Vx	4 responses, 1 CR

Expansion, optimism and **growth** take place. This attracts **better conditions. Legal matters** should benefit from this. Relationships with **in-laws** are good or should improve. **Religious** or **philosophical** matters are often of great interest. You are more open to **foreign cultures** and **people**. There may be increased opportunities and **luck** in your life. The **lottery** could be lucky for you now. **Travel** helps expand your life.

One man was in the army. He was sent to a university (Jupiter) for special training, which he described as giving him a "much better life than before." Another got a job in a carnival and traveled. A third person got a settlement from an insurance company from a car accident.

p Vx trine n Sturn   15 responses, 0 CR

You can gain the **respect** of others through your work, **discipline** and sense of **responsibility**. Some **finish paying** mortgage payments with this. If you are married, you can **stabilize** your present marriage if it has not been on firm ground. If dating, you may be attracted to **someone older** or very serious. Some may get the **rewards** of past effort.

One started orthodontic treatments (Saturn). Another received her law degree. A 23-year-old was thrown out of her parent's home because she was rebellious and on drugs. A fourth person, a teenager, was given a position of responsibility.

p Vx trine n Uranus   15 responses, 3 CR

This may bring **unexpected opportunities** or activities. You may make **new friends** or, at least, come in contact with **new ideas. Humanitarian activities** with groups may be undertaken, perhaps in **volunteer work**. There can be an **unexpected romance** with someone who is **unique** and interesting. You can relish the new **freedom** you have in your life.

One person decided on science (Uranus) as his college major. One 49-year-old man bought his present home (Uranus in his fourth), and, though married, fell in love with a new friend (not an affair). He said this woman opened his eyes to many things. He credits her with saving his life.

p Vx trine n Neptune   13 responses, 2 CR

One can choose to express this energy in the pursuit of **beauty, music, art** or one's **ideals,** or one can take the line of least resistance and **live in a fog** of drugs, alcohol, confusion or chaos. It is a time to pursue **spiritual matters** rather than material ones. **Intuitive insight, sensitivity** and **compassion** can be developed. Often a **psychic sense** is strong guiding the person in the right way.

One person began studying piano which was a major interest for many years. One began reading fantasy novels. Another filed for divorce from her alcoholic husband, no longer being his enabler.

p Vx trine n Pluto   18 responses, 3 CR

A person enters a **new phase** of his life. New paths are **opening up,** and one has enormous **power** to achieve new goals. One can **achieve** almost anything he wants while Pluto is so beneficial as long as she is willing to **let go of the past. Research** and **investigation** are favored. Some may help the elderly or others with their **finances.**

This was in my own chart at the time I was researching the Vertex (Pluto—research). Two boys, ages 10 and 11, became highly aware of girls (Pluto—sex). One person lost her much-loved cat that she had had for many years. Another got a good job with an insurance company (Pluto—insurance). A 33-year-old man formed a business with a chiropractor for rehabilitation. His Vertex is in Capricorn—business.

p Vx trine n Ascendant   27 responses, 2 CR

p Ascendant trine n Vx   28 responses, 5 CR

Unless other aspects contradict, **life goes smoothly, optimism** is high, and a person **feels good** about himself. One has **more confidence** than usual, and an **element of luck,** the luck that comes from a **confident**, optimistic attitude, seems to be present.

A 28-year-old woman with her Ascendant in Cancer (motherhood and family) had just received the results of an ultra sound and learned that her baby's heart development was normal. This relieved her anxiety since her two previous babies had died due to heart defects.

p Vx trine n Midheaven   8 responses, 1 CR

p Midheaven trine n Vx   24 responses, 4 CR

Career changes or changes in one's role in life are beneficial. The community you live in may be helpful. People met at this time may lead you into a direction that **brings fulfillment** in your life. Your **parents** may experience beneficial events or circumstances.

A 12-year-old girl said that she met a girl when this aspect was nearly exact who became a catalyst in bringing into form her artistic and writing skills. For the next 12 months the two worked together on a book they wrote and the subject illustrated. This eventually led to a degree in commercial art with a minor in English, a job with a newspaper doing graphics, copy for promotional ads, and brochures.

p Vx trine n Vx   3 responses, 1 CR

This seems to be **favorable**, but the number of responses is much too small to draw any conclusions.

One said this timed the beginning of a relationship. He took a course in country and western dance because he liked this type of dancing. The other one also had a big romance, which ended on good terms. He took a trip to Atlanta with this girl friend to visit his daughter's family.

Quincunxes

By analyzing and dissecting, one sees a need to re-assemble his energies before they can be used for his benefit. Therefore, it is an aspect of adjustment. It can bring a nagging problem that operates over an extended period of time. Health matters that have been building for some time can manifest. Like the opposition, it can be a separative aspect if the adjustments are not made.

p Vx quincunx n Sun	17 responses, 1 CR
p Sun quincunx n Vx	14 responses, 2 CR

Serious **health problems** can occur if one has several quincunxes, and quincunxes are present at the times when one is **affected by deaths** along with other indications. **Accidents and career moves** require **adjustments**. Some of the adjustments come because of being **laid off from work or changing jobs**.

One woman's husband was drafted into the Navy. The family moved to Guam requiring many adjustments. A 69-year-old man was diagnosed with colon and bladder cancer and severe emphysema. He had surgery, chemotherapy, and radiation. As a result he became much closer to his children. His Vertex is in Virgo and is the apex of a yod.

p Vx quincunx n Moon	14 responses, 0 CR
p Moon quincunx n Vx	7 responses, 1 CR

Adjustments are required because of **changes within the family**. These changes can be the **birth of a child**, the **illness** of a family member and his **need for care**, a **divorce** or **death** in the family, or any other kind of change among the family members. Most of these events are **emotional**, and they may include **changes** that take place or need to take place **at work**.

One 3-year-old became aware that she was different (gay). A 7-year-old got "dog worms" on her legs. The worms crawled around under the skin. She had to get 15 treatments to get them burned. For this same girl, her brother began having seizures. She was his main buddy since both of her parents were professional people. Her Vertex is in Virgo (health). It is the apex of a T-square to the fourth and Midheaven (parents). Her Moon is in Aquarius, which rules the calves of the legs.

p Vx quincunx n Mercury	20 responses, 4 CR
p Mercury quincunx n Vx	18 responses, 3 CR

Work, study and **education** are prominent with this aspect. One **began studying astrology**, one studying for **medical school**, and one for **pre-engineering. Respiratory illnesses** and **allergies** occurred. Adjustments are sometimes needed in one's **attitudes toward education**, some balancing education with other areas of their lives and others making education a priority.

One woman could not get colleges in the U.S.A. to acknowledge her training, which took place in several foreign countries, so she could not enter college. During the time this was in effect, she also lived through two earthquakes and a revolt in Monterrey, Mexico. All these events required adjustments.

p Vx quincunx n Venus	18 responses, 2 CR
p Venus quincunx n Vx	17 responses, 1 CR

You may **compromise** more than necessary toward others. **Difficulties** can come in **marriage** or **romance**. You do **favors** to **gain** their appreciation and to **keep peace** but then resent having to do them later. Concerns about your own **attractiveness** and **money problems** can arise. It could bring health problems pertaining to the **throat** or **veins.**

A 36-year-old teacher filed for divorce (Venus). She got a summer job to help with finances, but her home air conditioner went out. The repairs took all of her salary (Venus) that summer. Also when school started, she changed her teaching assignment and had to make adjustments for that too.

p Vx quincunx n Mars	12 responses, 2 CR
p Mars quincunx n Vx	7 responses, 2 CR

This aspect requires **adjustments** in one's **activities** or **relationships**. Mars can bring contact with **young men, initiative, strength** and **endurance**. It stimulates **new ventures**. Negatively, it can bring **strife, accidents, cuts, fires, rapes** (with other indications too) and **violence** in the life. More constructively, one could work with **machinery** or serve in the **military**.

An 8-year-old girl had repeated attacks of appendicitis in 1929, which were misdiagnosed. She had an increasing spread of infection (Mars). The situation was very critical before and after surgery (Mars). Mars rules her sixth and first houses, the houses of health.

p Vx quincunx n Jupiter	10 responses, 2 CR
p Jupiter quincunx n Vx	3 responses, 0 CR

Optimism, expansion, travel, education and **spiritual growth** all characterize this aspect, but it is a quincunx, so the usual **adjustments** have to be made to the changes. Parents having to adjust to children going off to **college**, and resorting to the **law** to **settle disputes** are two possibilities. **Health** problems relating to the **liver** or **overindulgence** are possible.

For a 42-year-old single woman her son's (Vertex in the fifth and the fifth ruled by Jupiter) graduation from college (Jupiter—natural ruler of colleges) came at this time. It was a happy event for her, but now her goals and priorities had to change.

p Vx quincunx n Saturn   15 responses, 1 CR

Quincunxes to the taskmaster, Saturn, are usually **difficult**. **Health problems** are often a concern. **Promotions** in the career come with **long hours** or **added responsibility**. Children could find their **schoolwork difficult** or their **teachers unsympathetic**. **Authority figures** could oppose one's ideas. **Money** could be tight.

One 36-year-old man began freelancing (Saturn—natural ruler of career), which led to his present career success in films (Vertex in Pisces in the sixth, Saturn in the second). He received a second Emmy a couple years later. He began a time of much long-distance travel. Natally, his Vertex is trine Saturn in the second bringing money.

p Vx quincunx n Uranus   15 responses, 1 CR

You can **expect the unexpected** with Uranus quincunxes. Your **freedom** and **independence** can increase or decrease. Some become their **own boss** assuring more **freedom**. You might work with the **airline industry** or work with **computers**. Some make unexpected **moves**. Young mothers may feel a great need for a **night out**.

A 7-year-old girl wrote a paper in school about wanting to be an airline stewardess (Uranus). She also had her first communion (Vertex in Sagittarius), a significant event for Catholics in general.

p Vx quincunx n Neptune   18 responses, 3 CR

You may not be **seeing** things as **clearly** as usual. Situations may seem **more glamorous** than they are. It's helpful for **musicians, artists, filmmakers, psychics** or anyone looking for **escape**. Unfortunately, this includes **drug** and **alcohol usage**. The period can be **confused** or **chaotic.** You or a friend or loved one could be in a **hospital.**

For one girl, her mother was drinking heavily and had to be put in a hospital. Another lived through a tornado bringing chaos into his life, and another got a new job as a pharmacist (Neptune).

p Vx quincunx n Pluto   13 responses, 3 CR

Drastic actions and **changes** can occur under the quincunx of Pluto. **"Either-or"** situations often result being either very good or very bad. **Power struggles** and **control issues** are not uncommon, and, in extreme cases, **deaths** in the person's environment occur.

A 41-year-old woman flew to California to help a girlfriend move out of her house. While there she lived through a 7.0 earthquake (Pluto). Pluto is in her 1st house in generous Leo.

p Vx quincunx n Ascendant   37 responses, 6 CR

p Ascendant quincunx n Vx   30 responses, 1 CR

Health matters often surface. **Strain** and **work problems** as well as **separations** manifest if the needed **adjustments** cannot be made. **Nagging problems** that have been **ignored** in the past now demand attention.

A 30-year-old woman's husband was traveling overseas much of the time. She was "stuck at home with the baby." She started building her own friendships and hobbies. There were many adjustments. Her Vertex is in the seventh (husband) and the progressed Ascendant (herself) was in Aries.

p Vx quincunx n Midheaven   0 responses

70

p Midheaven quincunx n Vx   19 responses, 1 CR

Work and **health** concerns predominate at this time. There can be **deaths** in one's circle. An **analysis** of present situations can show one where **adjustments** need to be made with **parents** or the **career**. Sometimes there is **dissatisfaction** with one's job making **changes necessary**.

One woman was finishing her college degree (Vertex in Sagittarius) and doing student teaching. She got her first teaching position during this time too, and, as a result, had many adjustments to make in both the career and her home life.

Oppositions

While oppositions generally show a need to balance both ends of the polarity by neglecting neither one of them, Vertex oppositions are somewhat unique. This is because an opposition to the Vertex is a conjunction to the AntiVertex. It is less self-blocking than a square, but there is still much tension created by this need to balance both ends shown by the signs and houses involved. One might think of this polarity like a marriage (Libra) where both a person's own wishes, needs, and desires must be met as well as the other person's wishes, needs, or desires. Neglecting either doesn't work.

Since the AntiVertex falls on the eastern side of the chart, the opposition to the Vertex throws the spotlight on the person himself, but the need to balance with the Vertex (others) is still present.

Like all oppositions, awareness of both ends of the polarity is strong, affording an opportunity to complete one's own personality from what the aspect teaches. Sometimes the aspect brings separations. As long as we avoid projecting our own needs

(AntiVertex) on the other person (Vertex), oppositions with the Vertex can be constructive.

p Vx opposition n Sun   13 responses, 2 CR

p Sun opposition n Vx   8 responses, 0 CR

Important events involving the **men** in one's life may occur. There is an urge to **increase** your own **feeling of importance**. Women, or any person, who had previously been under the domination of men in their lives now become more **confident** and **self-assertive**. A person can become a manager rather than being managed.

One 59-year-old woman's daughter (Sun—natural ruler of the fifth) had a brain tumor and died. The Sun rules her twelfth house of hospitals and sorrow, and, being the eighth house from the fifth, this brought her daughter's death. The progressed Vertex was in Cancer, the family, by this time.

p Vx opposition n Moon   5 responses, 0 CR

p Moon opposition n Vx   5 responses, 0 CR

Health and **family concerns** may surface, especially if a person does not balance his **emotional needs** with those of others. Sometimes being in **public life** satisfies this need. **New family members** need to be **assimilated** into the family. For some, there are family members who need their **care**.

A 36-year-old woman's mother was seriously ill. The woman quit teaching since she was very discontent with her job and needed to care for her mother. By the time this aspect was exact, she was very worried about whether she had made the right decision or not. Her Moon rules the tenth (her mother and her career).

p Vx opposition n Mercury	11 responses, 3 CR
p Mercury opposition n Vx	9 responses, 1 CR

Travel, learning or **teaching** others occurs now often with some opposition from others. Also, look at the houses ruled and tenanted by Mercury. Any **communication** or **means of communication** can be activated. Ideas could be **challenged**, or they need to be **balanced** with others' ideas.

A 41-year-old woman finished work on a college degree. Her father had financed her schooling. Her husband wanted her to go to work, causing some tension (she had several children). She had to balance home duties with other obligations. Mercury had progressed to the second and the natal Vertex is in the eighth (money and support). This aspect was present when the Federal Building in Oklahoma City was bombed.

p Vx opposition n Venus	14 responses, 1 CR
p Venus opposition n Vx	5 responses, 1 CR

Love relationships can be important, though sometimes challenging. If the proper balance is achieved, they can usually be **worked out**. Problems with the **throat** or **voice** can manifest. One may have different ideas of **beauty** or **social activity** from another.

A 9-year-old girl's mother remarried. She also had her tonsils (Venus) removed. Venus co-rules her tenth and rules her fourth of parents.

p Vx opposition n Mars	10 responses, 0 CR
p Mars opposition n Vx	4 responses, 0 CR

This brings an urge or need for **physical activity** whether in

sports, an **exercise program** or in the **police** or **armed forces.** Another person can block initiative. **Surgery** is a possibility, or one may have a **defiant, aggressive** attitude. You may be the person in an organization who gets a lot done and thereby **attracts criticism.**

One young woman had a break up with her lover (Mars rules young men—Vertex in the fifth). Since she had lost touch with friends and lived alone, she was lonely.

p Vx opposition n Jupiter   10 responses, 2 CR

The **optimism, generosity** and **expansion** of Jupiter may have to be balanced by other concerns. **Travel, higher education, publishing** and **religious concerns** enter the life. Disputes may have to be settled in the **courts. Travel** could broaden one's outlook.

One person had multiple Jupiter experiences. Her grandmother died (Jupiter rules the first of grandparents). Her mother-in-law (Jupiter) moved closer to this woman's family since she had liver cancer (the liver is ruled by Jupiter), so she took her for chemotherapy treatments. Her belief system was expanding (Jupiter) and she traveled (Jupiter) to several conferences.

p Vx opposition n Saturn   8 responses, 0 CR

Awareness of one's **limitations** and **duties** comes to the fore. Some events at this time are **difficult** or **sorrowful** in some way. New **responsibilities** may be **unwanted,** but growth comes from meeting them. One's **health** may not be up to par.

One man said that his father (Saturn) wanted him to play football when the subject was 11 years old. He didn't want to. He wanted to run away but couldn't. Saturn was in the 1st and the Vertex had progressed to the seventh.

p Vx opposition n Uranus   3 responses

This aspect may bring **rebelliousness** or an **awareness** of and **interest** in **new technologies**. One may be drawn to the **sciences** or **aviation**. **Personal freedom** is a must, and either stressful friendships or new **friendships** bring one in contact with new, exciting things. It is a good time to study **astrology**, especially in **groups**.

One 10-year-old became very interested in video games and sports. She also became more rebellious than usual.

p Vx opposition n Neptune   8 responses, 1 CR

his energy may be used to seek **beauty** and inspiration through the **arts**, or **service** as in the **medical fields**, working with the **poor, downtrodden** or **handicapped**. Negatively one may choose **drugs, alcohol** or other forms of **escape**. **Indecision** is often a problem, or the aspect can bring **confusion, chaos, deception** or charitable **compassion**.

One young woman was in medical school. Her Vertex in Aquarius drew her to the sciences.

p Vx opposition n Pluto   8 responses, 3 CR

One may be very **determined** to succeed which can result in **power struggles**. Something that is no longer needed can be **purged** from the life. **Intense emotions** and **sexual feelings** may meet opposition. **Money** belonging to others, **loans, mortgage payments, insurance** or **taxes** can be of concern.

One woman changed her major in college at the time this aspect was in effect (her Vertex is in Sagittarius) causing her life to go in a different direction. For a four-year-old, his dog died causing great sorrow (Pluto in the twelfth). His Vertex had progressed to his 6th of small animals.

p Vx opposition n Ascendant   15 responses, 3 CR

p Ascendant opposition n Vx   15 responses, 2 CR

This is often one of the most **traumatic times** of a person's life. You have to work **something out with another person**. For married people, there can be a **divorce** or at least a **major difference** that needs to be worked out. For single people of appropriate age, there can be a **marriage**. There could be a major problem with a **business partner**.

One man said that when he was a boy of six, he felt he had to earn his father's attention. His father saw him differently than he really was. This was the beginning of lifelong problems with his father.

p Vx opposition n Midheaven   1 response, 0 CR

p Midheaven opposition n Vx   0 responses, 0 CR

This occurs very rarely and then only for people whose Vertex moves very fast. One response is not enough to make generalizations.

For the one example we have, the woman and her husband took a trip to Europe where they met her son and his wife in London for a week of sightseeing. Her Vertex is in the fifth house (children) in the sign of Sagittarius (foreign travel).

5

Rectification with the Vertex

The Vertex is a very useful tool for rectification when the time of a birth is approximate. Since rectification must come from timed factors in the chart, only the Ascendant, Midheaven, Part of Fortune, and the Vertex may be used. For example, the Sun conjunct Venus may be a pleasant aspect to have, but it says nothing about the time of day a person was born. Rectification takes all the tools the astrologer can muster. The more skills she can use, the better her chances are of arriving at the correct time.

We must admit that some people make better subjects for rectification than others. Some people have had very few major events, especially very young people. I try to get subjects to list about ten of the most important events in their lives. Often it helps if details of these events are given. Usually giving the time of each event as "early September" or "mid-August" and the year is sufficient, but exact dates are even better.

I find that negative or difficult events work better than the positive ones. This may make it seem that we take a negative approach to life, but actually, since negative events usually require action on the subject's part, the event is more vivid. Some subjects have a better memory for details than others, and often it is some small detail that gives us a clue.

I had worked for a long time on a woman's chart that had either a Gemini or Cancer Ascendant according to the approximate time she gave me. Nothing seemed to work since one of the main events I was using was the death of her father. Finally, one day she casually mentioned that it was as though her father had died three years earlier because he had worked for the railroad and, three years before he died, he somehow was gassed from some fumes from the locomotive. She said he was "like a vegetable" from that day on. Using that date as his death date along with a very strong Neptune (gasses) activation, everything fell into place giving her a 29 Gemini Ascendant.

Clues About the Birthtime

Usually clients will have some clues about their birthtimes. We hear things like, "it was in the morning," "the family had just finished dinner," or "it was still dark outside," or any clue will help you narrow it down. For the person who has no clue at all, rectification is almost impossible. A one-hour leeway is about the most an astrologer can handle. Thirty minutes is much better.

Determining the Ascendant Sign

When the astrologer has a fairly narrow time to work with, he needs to check to see which Ascendants are possible within that time span. If there are two or more possibilities (i.e., Aries or Taurus) looking at the subject's physical appearance can help. Generally speaking, the fixed sign Ascendants (Taurus, Leo, Scorpio, and Aquarius) are large people. They are stout and robust, and when overweight seem more "big" rather than "fat." They are often deep chested. Cancer and Pisces tend more toward fatness (or they gain weight easily), yet they too are stout and robust. Aries, Gemini, and Sagittarius are more the tall, thin types, while Virgo and Capricorn are short, thin types. Libra seems to be in a group by itself. Usually they are beautiful and balanced, but they do tend to gain weight as they get older. Practice will make one more aware of these characteristics.

People tend to look like their Ascendant sign even more than their Sun signs unless the Sun is part of a stellium. It is the Ascendant sign that we need for rectification, so it is helpful to determine which sign is most like the person's appearance. You will find many exceptions, though, and these descriptions are quite appropriate for some but totally off the mark for others. Be flexible. However, in a general way, the following descriptions can be useful.

Factors That Vary the Appearance

Few people fit these descriptions exactly. There are several factors that vary the appearance:

- Planets rising in the sign on the Ascendant will modify the appearance.

- The sign that the ruler of the Ascendant is located in may modify the appearance.

- If the Moon's North Node is on the Ascendant, the person tends to be taller than expected; if the South Node is on the Ascendant, she tends to be shorter.

- A strong stellium will have an influence on the appearance.

- Sometimes the positions of Jupiter and Saturn will enlarge that portion of the body (Jupiter) or tend to shrink it (Saturn).

The body parts that are ruled by the signs are:

Aries: head
Taurus: neck
Gemini: arms and shoulders
Cancer: breasts and stomach

Leo: heart and upper back
Virgo: abdomen and intestines
Libra: kidneys, lower back
Scorpio: sexual organs
Sagittarius: thighs
Capricorn: knees
Aquarius: calves, ankles
Pisces: feet
When the Ascendant is in:

Aries

- A person is apt to have a convex profile (like Capricorn) and a triangular shaped face.

- Lacking persistence, they start more than they finish.

- The eyebrows grow all the way across (like Scorpio), and two vertical lines form between the eyes.

- The mouth is full and wide and is flanked by grooves in the cheeks. The chin is narrow.

- They tend to lean forward and to walk energetically.

- They are outspoken, critical, bossy, and tactless but do not hold a grudge.

- They have strong, deep commanding voices.

- They are lean, dry, muscular, and wiry.

- The hair is plentiful but rough, wiry, and unruly.

- Aries Ascendant men often have a conspicuous Adam's apple.

Taurus
- They have a square-shaped head and often have dimples.

- The brow and compact nose are close to the plane of the face. The bearing is stately, dignified, and proud.

- They are rugged and solid, yet have great beauty.

- Luxuriant hair often grows down in a peak on the forehead.

- They have a full, short neck and broad and heavy shoulders. The head seems to sit on the shoulders.

- The torso is solid flesh, not fat, being longer and larger in proportion to the extremities.

- The eyes are small under arched brows with heavy eyelids giving a mild expression.

- If weight is gained, it fills out the whole body, not just the abdomen.

- They like to stay put, so they are hard to rouse and hard to stop.

- They resent being rushed because they want to finish things beautifully and perfectly.

Gemini
- They have a moderately convex profile.

- There is great height to the forehead.

- They may have "Gemini bumps" just below the hairline, like corners to the upper forehead.

- The body is tall and slender and usually stays that way.

- The light and wavy hair thins out before it gets gray.

- The shoulders are not wide and slope a little.

- There is a tense look about the relatively thin lips but seldom a sour expression.

- The expression is quick and bird-like with eyes that are in constant motion.

- The muscles are of the long, enduring kind rather than the bunchy, sudden-effort kind.

- The eyes are the width of a full eye apart and brightly alert.

Cancer

- They have large heads and short bodies that tend to grow fat.

- The forehead has a distinct outward bulge.

- The ears are small and the eyes are large, round, and dreamy with upper lids that are heavy. The lips are full. The women tend to be heavy-breasted.

- Some are thin and bony (like Capricorn) with small eyes and thin lips.

- They are changeable like the moon but have constancy and tenacity.

- They're loyal to and proud of their families.

- They love a good cry, tend to be jealous, and, when in one of their "moods" they crawl into their shell.

- The skin is pale or sallow.

- Even if fat they are active.

- They walk in the rolling gait of a sailor or with a sidling-crablike motion.

Leo

- The chest is heavier than the hips, which are lion-like or narrow. The body is cone shaped-a "carrot-on-end."

- The muscles are well developed in the young.

- The hair is fine, curly, and mane-like, often looking like a halo.

- When weight is gained, it is distributed above the waistline. Even when fat, they do not seem to be fat so much as big and strong.

- The face is fair or ruddy; the shoulders are broad; the back is strong.

- The chin is definite but rounded; the lips are full; the lower lip is inclined to protrude; the upper lip is abrupt from the nose.

- After early youth the tissues of the face sag away from the nostrils to the corners of the mouth in curtain-like curves.

- The head is large (like Cancer), round, and flat behind. The men are often bald.

- Another type of Leo has a dark vitality in the face and an unobtrusive, almost mousy manner.

Virgo

- They have a long head and neck with a large forehead and small chin.

- The lips are seldom full with the upper one long from the base of the nose to the mouth.

- The women are often beautiful due to having the right proportions, and both sexes are usually photogenic.

- The hips and shoulders are broader than Gemini's.

- The face is seldom fleshy, but the hips are in later life.

- The eyes have a full upper lid; the nose looks sharp.

- The body is short, thin and angular but well built.

- The face is pale and smooth with fine features.

- The voice is soft and matter-of-fact, and they have a tendency to talk to themselves.

- They walk with a smooth, plain tread, although some may be crippled, scarred, or marked.

Libra

- Libra features are balanced, not "overdone." No one feature stands out.

- The face and body are based on curves.

- The skin is beautifully clear, even into old age, with a fine pink color in later life.

- The hair grows low on the forehead.

- The lips are full and shaped like a Cupid's bow"; the voice is soft and melodic.

- Dimples often appear in the cheek or chin.

- Libras, especially the women, tend to curve in the lumbar section of the spine, and the walk is lively with a dancing tread.

- The nose is not large, nor irregular, but shapely with delicate nostrils.

- They are usually tall and slender in youth but grow heavier with age.

- The mouth has a short upper lip and teeth like pearls.

Scorpio
- They are big-boned, deep-chested types with a strong body and steady, piercing eyes.

- The skin is reddish and dusky. Often the hair has reddish highlights too.

- The hair grows low on the forehead, which can be quite high itself.

- The eyebrows very often meet above the nose, which has a high and noticeable humped, bony bridge and dips at the tip.

- The brows have a Mephistophelean, sardonic sharp outer corner.

- The ears are large; the mouth (like Pisces) has a droop at the outer corners; the lower lip is full and reddish.

- The cheekbones are high; the jaw is wide and strong, and the walk is lizard-like or a duck walk. They are hip swingers.

- The neck is full and, while not as short as Taurus, looks just as strong.

- Compared to others of the same sex in their families, they are short to medium.

- Heavy women of this sign are buxom, shapely and active.

Sagittarius

- They're usually tall and slender with a tendency to have stooping shoulders.

- The nose is aquiline and slightly humped; the ears tend to stick out; the upper lip is long.

- For the men the hair, though abundant and wavy, retreats above the temples, first leaving a tuft in the center and finally leaving the entire upper forehead bare.

- The jaw and chin are long, the mouth bowed, and the eyes are round and alert.

- The lashes and brows tend to be darker than the hair.

- The legs are long and used for much walking, with a hip swing, like Scorpio but faster with longer strides.

- The face is convex (or "horse-faced") with a long, protruding chin.

- They like new scenes, travel, and sports.

- He is no fireside sitter, and he tends to sit with his toes turned inward.

- They are extremely talkative (Gemini is a close second) and jovial. They chuckle when they laugh.

Capricorn

- They are usually short and bony, especially about the knees, which swing out a little, being most noticeable when running.

- The boniness is apparent in the face structure also, which has small features. The head is large, skull bony, hair thin, profile convex, nose aquiline, face long and thin, and forehead relatively low.

- The brow area often overhangs above eyes that are usually close together. The nose is sharp with a dip.

- The mouth is thin and small, and the neck is thin and skinny.

- Usually the upper frame is heavier than the lower (like Leo), the legs slender and the shins quite often skinny with small calves.

- Capricorn Ascendant people seem older than their years in youth but younger than their generation when older.

- The walk is a strut, lordly and stalking.

- The chin is strong but narrow; the skin is generally drawn tight over the bones.

- They're inclined to be quiet, deep thinking, cautious and dependable.

- The eyes are deep-seated, cold, with an expression that is quiet, serious, and tired-looking.

Aquarius

- There are probably a larger number of beautiful or handsome people with an Aquarian Ascendant than any other (Libra and Gemini run a close second and third).

- Their heads are the square type in both front view and in profile; the voice is loud.

- There is a characteristic line or curl-up of the flesh at the outer corners of the eyes, especially for the Uranian types, which tend to be tall; the Saturn types are short.

- The body and the face are built on lines and geometrical masses, not curves.

- The wavy hair is fine and thin, the forehead is high and parallel with the back of the head, and the nose is well chiseled but small.

- The mouth is sharply defined and the chin definite, though not large.

- The bones are well covered with firm flesh, with no dimples.

- The glance is alert and penetrating in a way different from Scorpio, less secretive, more impersonal. They have laughing eyes.

- There is a "delta" or prominence, between the brows, above the root of the nose.

- The shoulders are broad and square, the joints noticeable, the calf bulge high, and the ankles weak.

- There is usually a tendency for the women to lack the usual body curves expected of the sex.

Pisces

- They have plentiful, thick hair that is disorderly and will not stay put.

- The head is small with hair that makes it seem large; the complexion is pale to pasty.

- The nose is short, small, joining the brow with very little indentation.

- The ears are round, soft and flabby.

- The nicely rounded chin doubles and sometimes triples.

- The neck is short, soft and full.

- The mouth is fine, sensitive, and winsome; the corners droop; the voice is soft, deep, and silent.

- The eyes have heavy upper lids with a down dropping line at the outer corners and sometimes a fish-like stare.

- The arms and legs are short and small; the hands and feet are small, wide, and drop-shaped, as are the nails; the walk is fluidic, dreamy, and meandering.

- They have short plump bodies that are watery fat, with soft fleshy tissues, round shoulders with very wide hips. They dance well even when fat.

Planets Close to the Ascendant or Midheaven

When you've narrowed the Ascendant down to a decanate (or even two decanates, which is better than three), look to see which planets could be close to the Midheaven or the IC before or after the cusp. Since the Midheaven is the angle that moves closest to one degree a year by secondary progression, it is a good one to use to estimate the time.

If Saturn is close, ask the subject if there was a time that represented a hardship, a restriction, or difficult time for the person or his parents early in life. If Mars is close, ask if there was an accident, a surgery, a period of strife, or a very active period. If Uranus is close, was there a sudden, unexpected event. If Venus is close, a happy event such as the birth of a child, a wedding, or the addition of some luxury to her life, etc.

Give the chart a speculative Midheaven or IC that is the number of degrees from the angle as the age of the person when that event or time occurred. Some events involve a period of time rather than a specific time, but get it as close as possible.

Further Narrowing the Ascendant

When you have determined the probable sign of the Ascendant within the approximate time frame you've been given, it is then time to try to narrow the field further.

First, using the decanates, try to narrow the Ascendant degree to one of the three decanates. The first decanate of each sign is the sign itself. The second decanate is the next sign of the same element, and the third decanate is the sign of the second sign of the same element. So we have the following:

Aries 1st, Aries	2nd - Leo	3rd - Sagittarius
Taurus 1st, Taurus	2nd - Virgo	3rd - Capricorn
Gemini 1st, Gemini	2nd - Libra	3rd - Aquarius
Cancer 1st, Cancer	2nd - Scorpio	3rd - Pisces
Leo 1st, Leo	2nd - Sagittarius	3rd - Aries
Virgo 1st, Virgo	2nd - Capricorn	3rd - Taurus
Libra 1st, Libra	2nd - Aquarius	3rd - Gemini
Scorpio 1st, Scorpio	2nd - Pisces	3rd - Cancer
Sagittarius 1st, Sagittarius	2nd - Aries	3rd - Leo
Capricorn 1st, Capricorn	2nd - Taurus	3rd - Virgo
Aquarius 1st, Aquarius	2nd - Gemini	3rd - Libra
Pisces 1st, Pisces	2nd - Cancer	3rd - Scorpio

Matching the Ascendant, Midheaven, and Vertex Progressions to Events

Now it is time to begin matching the Ascendant, Midheaven, and Vertex progressions to the ten or so events your subject has provided you, or, better yet, ask the subject about possible events at the time of these progressions. I usually start with conjunctions since they are the strongest. I usually set up my computer to run Ascendant, Midheaven and Vertex conjunctions together or individually. Seldom are there a large number of them. You want both planets to the angles and angles to the planets.

When interpreting the aspects, remember to consider the houses ruled and tenanted by the planet as well as the nature of the planet. Also consider the natal aspects to that planet and note where they come from. If you find that some of them seem to be a year or more off, adjust the time so that they will more closely coincide. Generally, four minutes of time equals a year.

An Example

I was given the time within one-half hour for a man who wanted a rectification. After getting the time as close as I could based on his marriage time and a few other events, I checked with the man about the only two conjunctions or oppositions he had had of the Vertex during his life. If the time were correct there should be some important events at those times. The first one was the conjunction of the progressed Vertex to the seventh cusp. At that time he had met his present wife and they married a few months later although he said he knew when he met her that they would marry. The second one was the progressed Vertex opposing natal Neptune in the 2nd which was natally squared by Venus in the eleventh and Jupiter in the fifth. This time he lost a great deal of money (second house) through the bad advice of a friend (eleventh house) about a speculative (fifth house) venture.

6

The Vertex in Event Charts

In the charts of major events, one often finds the Vertex involved in a major configuration. For negative events, this could be a T-square or a grand cross. The configuration may be entirely in the event chart (the transit chart) or among the natal, progressed, and directed charts. The Vertex shows the fated nature of the event.

Attack on the United States

One such event is the attack on the United States in New York City on September 11, 2001. No one will ever forget this day when most of us heard from newscasters on our television set that America was being attacked. The chart for the time the first airliner hit the first of the Twin Towers in New York City shows very significant Vertex activity. Here the Vertex is the apex of an exact T-Square comprising Neptune in the fourth (our homeland or country) in opposition to the Part of Suicide (Asc + Jupiter - the twelfth cusp) at 6 Leo 20 in the tenth house. We see Neptune's influence in the fact that the enemy was very elusive and not even clearly defined since the enemy was a group of widely dispersed terrorists rather than a country with a recognized government, and, of course, the men who committed this act were committing suicide.

93

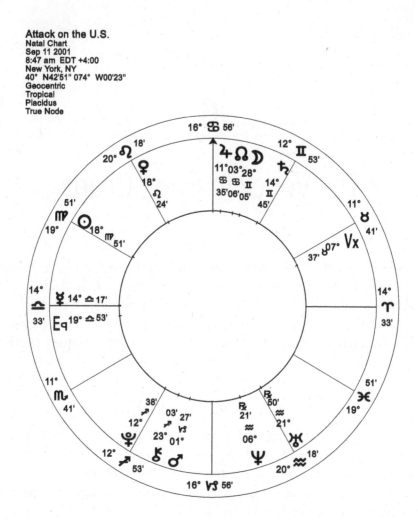

Attack on the U.S.
Natal Chart
Sep 11 2001
8:47 am EDT +4:00
New York, NY
40° N42'51" 074° W00'23"
Geocentric
Tropical
Placidus
True Node

Federal Building Bombing

Another event only slightly less horrifying was the bombing of the Federal Building in Oklahoma City, Oklahoma. Again we have significant Vertex activity. This time the Vertex is conjunct the North Node opposing Mercury square the Part of Fortune. The Part of Death in this chart (14 Gemini 10) is quincunx Jupiter, and the midpoint of Mars and Saturn (of death) at 3 Sagittarius 29 is also quincunx Mercury, the chart ruler. On this day, April 19,

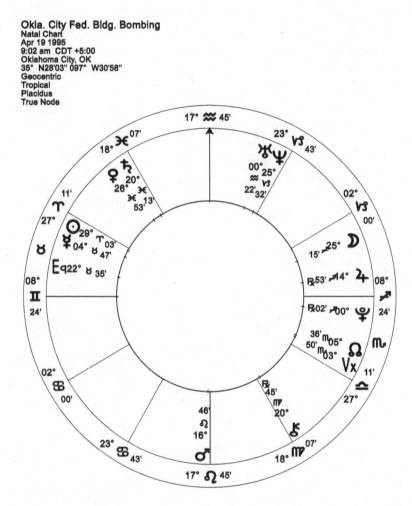

Okla. City Fed. Bldg. Bombing
Natal Chart
Apr 19 1995
9:02 am CDT +5:00
Oklahoma City, OK
35° N28'03" 097° W30'58"
Geocentric
Tropical
Placidus
True Node

1995, Timothy McVey and possibly others parked a van in front of the Federal Building with enough explosives to demolish most of the building and kill many people, including children.

Founding of the Third Reich

The establishment of The Third Reich in Nazi Germany unleashed many evils in the world. The chart for this event again reveals significant Vertex activity. This time it is part of a cardinal

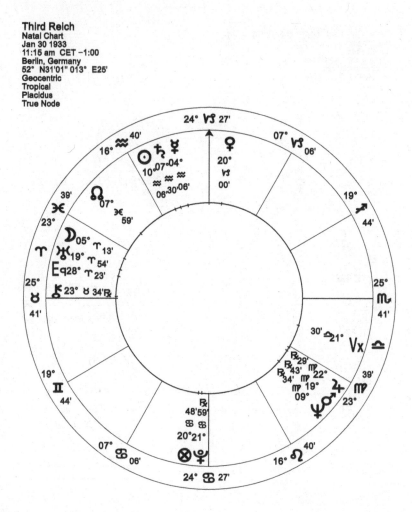

Third Reich
Natal Chart
Jan 30 1933
11:15 am CET −1:00
Berlin, Germany
52° N31'01" 013° E25'
Geocentric
Tropical
Placidus
True Node

grand cross in cadent houses. The chart ruler, Venus, is square the Vertex, opposition Pluto which is conjunct the Part of Fortune, and square Uranus in the twelfth house. Pluto as part of this grand cross indicates the greed for power by the organization, and Uranus, the negation of individuality and the rights of individuals. This organization was responsible for much of the terror experienced by Europeans, especially the Jews, during the war. It was one of the chief tools for Adolf Hitler to maintain his hold over several European countries and their peoples. It was not defeated completely until the end of the war in 1945, 12 years after its establishment.

Bombing of Pearl Harbor

A quadwheel of the United States (Sibley chart) with the progressed chart, the directed chart, and the event chart of the Attack on Pearl Harbor reveals multiple Vertex activity. First we find the progressed Sun in the 1st quincunx the natal Vertex and Part of Fortune. Then the progressed Vertex opposes transiting Saturn, the chart ruler of the event. Third, the directed Vertex is quincunx natal and progressed Uranus. While there are many other indications of this event, such as the previous solar eclipse (27 Virgo 47) conjunct progressed Neptune, showing the sneakiness of this attack, the Vertex activity should not be ignored.

Assassination of President Kennedy

The chart of John F. Kennedy's assassination shows the Vertex to be part of a yod since it is quincunx the natal Moon and sextile the North Node. Yods are frequently present in death charts.

The quadwheel of this event also shows multiple Vertex activations. The directed Vertex is conjunct natal Pluto, and transiting Mars is conjunct directed Pluto, both of which are square the natal Vertex which is in the eighth house of death. Since Pluto rules the underworld, this would tend to support, but not prove, the theory that the mob was somehow responsible for Kennedy's death. The transiting Vertex is conjunct directed Saturn, and directed Jupiter is conjunct the progressed Vertex. This is an unusually large number of Vertex aspects.

Even natally Kennedy's Vertex is conjunct violent Mars and Mercury, ruler of his ninth and twelfth houses of distant places

---

Vertex: The Third Angle

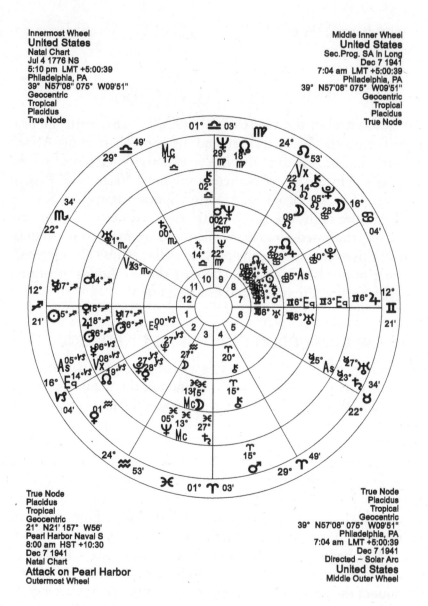

Innermost Wheel
United States
Natal Chart
Jul 4 1776 NS
5:10 pm LMT +5:00:39
Philadelphia, PA
39° N57'08" 075° W09'51"
Geocentric
Tropical
Placidus
True Node

Middle Inner Wheel
United States
Sec.Prog. SA In Long
Dec 7 1941
7:04 am LMT +5:00:39
Philadelphia, PA
39° N57'08" 075° W09'51"
Geocentric
Tropical
Placidus
True Node

True Node
Placidus
Tropical
Geocentric
21° N21' 157° W56'
Pearl Harbor Naval S
8:00 am HST +10:30
Dec 7 1941
Natal Chart
Attack on Pearl Harbor
Outermost Wheel

True Node
Placidus
Tropical
Geocentric
39° N57'08" 075° W09'51"
Philadelphia, PA
7:04 am LMT +5:00:39
Dec 7 1941
Directed – Solar Arc
United States
Middle Outer Wheel

and hidden enemies respectively. It makes a wide conjunction to Jupiter, a trine to the Moon showing his public support, and a square to Uranus, which indicates the sudden nature of his death.

98

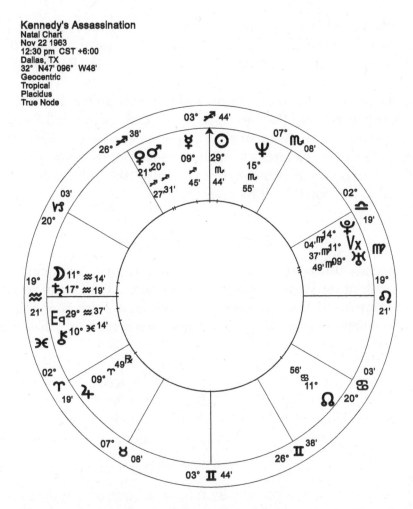

Kennedy's Assassination
Natal Chart
Nov 22 1963
12:30 pm CST +6:00
Dallas, TX
32° N47' 096° W48'
Geocentric
Tropical
Placidus
True Node

When the event chart of Kennedy's assassination is placed with the U.S. (Sibley) chart, showing the importance of this event to the country, the Vertex is again highly significant. It is placed in the ninth house of distant places square the Ascendant and Descendant. The previous solar eclipse was at 27 Cancer 24 conjunct the U.S. Vertex and Part of Fortune in the eighth opposite the U.S. Pluto. The country's fortunes were changed (Part of Fortune) through death (Pluto and eighth house).

The death of this charismatic 35th President ended the myth of "Camelot" in the United States. Never before (or since) had the President and his wife added so much glamour to the Presidency.

The causes of his assassination will probably always be controversial and obscure (Moon, ruler of the U.S. eighth and Saturn square Neptune in the event chart). In some way we will never understand this was a fated event that the nation needed to experience. The government's attempts to explain the event only seem to add to the distrust felt by many people.

Crash of the Concorde

Airline crashes, too, have strong Vertex activity. An example is the crash of the Concorde in Gonesse, France. The Concorde offered supersonic travel between Paris and New York saving time and reducing fatigue for its passengers since it took only half the time of a subsonic flight.

There is virtually no atmospheric turbulence at the very high altitudes at which it flies (18,000 meters/49,000 feet). The French Accident Investigation Bureau concluded that it was likely that a strip of metal found on the runway caused a split in the tire.

This statement did not wholly resolve the question of the cause of the crash, however, as the reasons why one engine failed and another was faulty remained unclear.

The Concorde crashed just after take off and the crash killed 113 people. All Concords were grounded but resumed flying November 7, 2001 after technical modifications. Here the previous solar eclipse at 10 Cancer 15 is conjunct the Vertex in the eighth of death quincunx Pluto and the Part of Travel by Air (Asc. + Uranus - the twelfth) at 8 Sagittarius 09. In addition, the

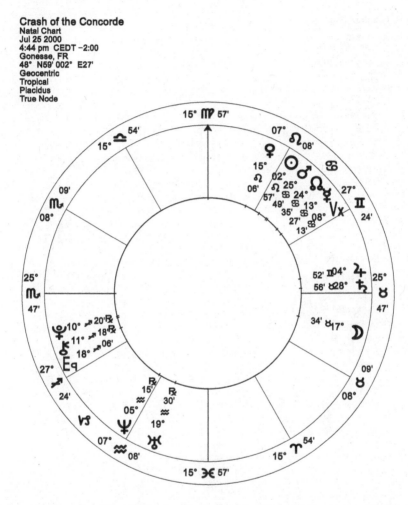

Crash of the Concorde
Natal Chart
Jul 25 2000
4:44 pm CEDT –2:00
Gonesse, FR
48° N59' 002° E27'
Geocentric
Tropical
Placidus
True Node

Mars/Saturn midpoint, which often signifies death, is exactly conjunct the eighth house.

Crash of Flight 800

A second example of an airline crash is the Crash of Flight 800 in Long Island, NY on July 17, 1996. Here the Vertex in the seventh opposes the Part of Death in the first at 23 Capricorn 46. It also quincunxes Uranus in the 1st and semi-sextiles the Part of

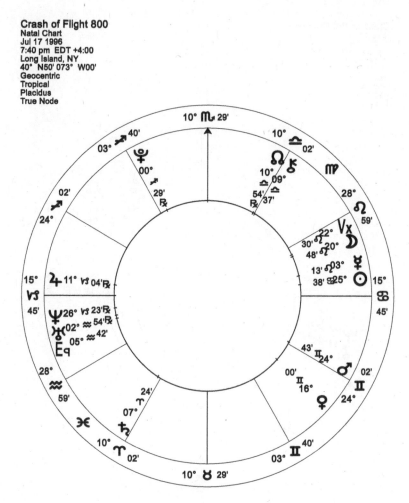

Crash of Flight 800
Natal Chart
Jul 17 1996
7:40 pm EDT +4:00
Long Island, NY
40° N50' 073° W00'
Geocentric
Tropical
Placidus
True Node

Travel by Air at 22 Virgo 53. Quincunxes are almost always present in death charts.

The Boeing 747-100 crashed into the Atlantic Ocean off the coast of Long Island shortly after takeoff from Kennedy International Airport. It was on a regularly scheduled flight to Paris, France. Witnesses saw an explosion and then debris falling to the ocean. There are no reports of the flight crew reporting a problem to air traffic control. The airplane was manufactured in November

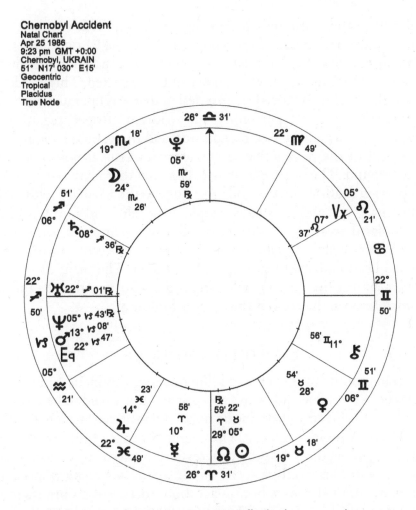

Chernobyl Accident
Natal Chart
Apr 25 1986
9:23 pm GMT +0:00
Chernobyl, UKRAIN
51° N17' 030° E15'
Geocentric
Tropical
Placidus
True Node

1971. It had accumulated about 93,303 flight hours and 16,869 cycles. On board the airplane were 212 passengers and 18 crew members. The airplane was destroyed and there were no survivors.

The Chernobyl Accident

The Chernobyl accident in the Soviet Union April 25, 1986, is another type of accident. Again we find the Vertex in the eighth house as the apex of a T-Square with Pluto (atomic energy and

death) in the tenth and the Sun in the fourth. This accident occurred the day before a lunar eclipse at 4 Scorpio 01 on Pluto. It is
also interesting that Uranus is conjunct the Ascendant of this chart
showing that the event was sudden and unexpected. This accident
was the result of a flawed reactor design that was operated with in-
adequately trained personnel and without proper regard for
safety. The resulting steam explosion and fire released about five
percent of the radioactive reactor core into the atmosphere and
downwind. Thirty people were killed, and there have since been
up to ten deaths from thyroid cancer due to the accident. In the following years, about 210,000 people were relocated into less con-
taminated areas. An authoritative UN report in 2000 confirmed
that there is no scientific evidence of any significant radiation-re-
lated health effects to most people exposed. The main casualties
were among firefighters, including those who attended the initial
small fires on the roof of the turbine building.

Sinking of the Titanic

The sinking of the Titanic killing many prominent Americans
has been the subject of books and movies. It was said to be unsink-
able, yet it hit an iceberg in the north Atlantic causing a major disaster in America's history. The overconfidence of Jupiter, placed
here conjunct the Vertex by progression, was a strong factor in the
tragedy since not only was the ship traveling at a reckless speed in
iceberg-infested waters but, in addition, there was an insufficient
number of lifeboats. Some people were saved, but too many were
not.

When we place this event chart in a quadwheel with the U.S.
chart, its progressions and directions for the time of the event, we
see the fated quality of the disaster. Directed Jupiter conjoins the
Vertex-Mercury conjunction in the eighth of the U.S. chart opposing Pluto in the second. Then a grand cross is formed by the previous solar eclipse at 27 Libra 38 conjunct progressed Saturn in the

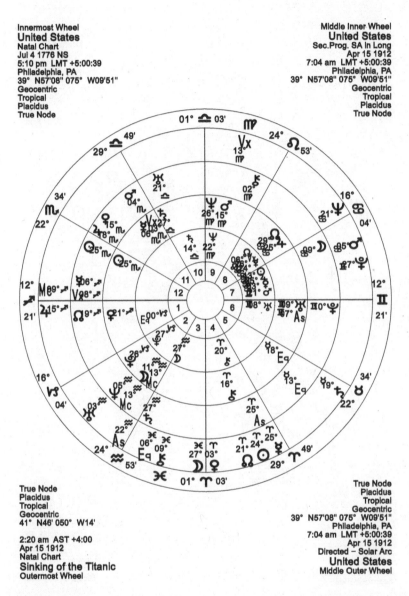

Innermost Wheel
United States
Natal Chart
Jul 4 1776 NS
5:10 pm LMT +5:00:39
Philadelphia, PA
39° N57'08" 075° W09'51"
Geocentric
Tropical
Placidus
True Node

Middle Inner Wheel
United States
Sec.Prog. SA In Long
Apr 15 1912
7:04 am LMT +5:00:39
Philadelphia, PA
39° N57'08" 075° W09'51"
Geocentric
Tropical
Placidus
True Node

True Node
Placidus
Tropical
Geocentric
41° N46' 050° W14'

2:20 am AST +4:00
Apr 15 1912
Natal Chart
Sinking of the Titanic
Outermost Wheel

True Node
Placidus
Tropical
Geocentric
39° N57'08" 075° W09'51"
Philadelphia, PA
7:04 am LMT +5:00:39
Apr 15 1912
Directed – Solar Arc
United States
Middle Outer Wheel

tenth opposing the Part of Death at 26 Aries 05 in the fourth. The coming solar eclipse of April 17, 1912, also opposes this Saturn and squares the natal Vertex-Mercury. No doubt the tragedy left permanent scars on the ones who were saved.

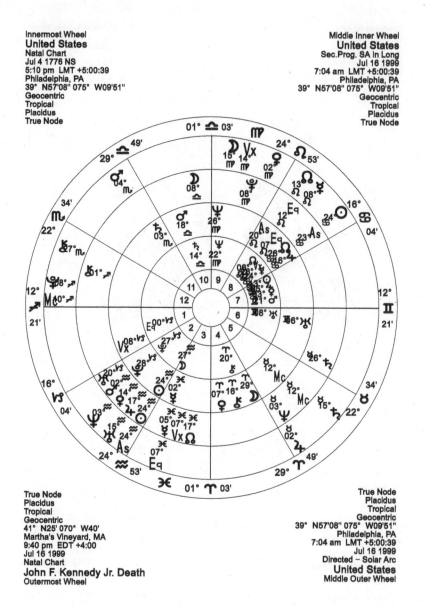

Innermost Wheel
United States
Natal Chart
Jul 4 1776 NS
5:10 pm LMT +5:00:39
Philadelphia, PA
39° N57'08" 075° W09'51"
Geocentric
Tropical
Placidus
True Node

Middle Inner Wheel
United States
Sec.Prog. SA in Long
Jul 16 1999
7:04 am LMT +5:00:39
Philadelphia, PA
39° N57'08" 075° W09'51"
Geocentric
Tropical
Placidus
True Node

True Node
Placidus
Tropical
Geocentric
41° N25' 070° W40'
Martha's Vineyard, MA
9:40 pm EDT +4:00
Jul 16 1999
Natal Chart
John F. Kennedy Jr. Death
Outermost Wheel

True Node
Placidus
Tropical
Geocentric
39° N57'08" 075° W09'51"
Philadelphia, PA
7:04 am LMT +5:00:39
Jul 16 1999
Directed – Solar Arc
United States
Middle Outer Wheel

Death of John F. Kennedy, Jr.

The death of John F. Kennedy, Jr. off Martha's Vineyard in 1999 again captured the sympathies of the nation. This was one more tragedy for a family that had known too much death. No doubt Kennedy was rather inexperienced to be flying in the bad weather of the day, but we do not know what prompted him to try the flight anyway with tragic results for himself as well as his wife, Carolyn Bissett Kennedy, and his sister-in-law.

Astrologically, there was an exact grand cross with the progressed Vertex in the ninth opposing Mercury in the third square natal Vertex in the fifth and the transiting Node in the eleventh. The previous lunar eclipse at 11 Leo 27 could be the trigger for this grand cross.

It is interesting, too, that the directed Moon, directed Chiron, and the progressed Part of Fortune are all conjunct the eighth cusp affecting both the seventh house (his wife) and the eighth (death). In addition, his directed Ascendant was conjunct his natal Part of Death which was 21 Libra 17.

Princess Diana's Fatal Accident

The death of Princess Diana came as a shock to the world. Many were so stunned that they refused to believe that it had happened when they first heard it. She was indeed the "People's Princess" who was greatly admired for the work she gave to several causes that helped relieve suffering in the world. The outpouring of grief after her death was perhaps the greatest we had seen in the century.

The divorced Princess was with the man who was rumored to soon be her fiancé, and a man who had been drinking was driving them from the hotel where they had dined. As might be expected, the transiting Vertex was conjunct natal and progressed Neptune (alcohol). The result was a major accident that killed all but one man who was in the front seat with the driver.

Transiting Uranus was conjunct natal Jupiter, her chart ruler,

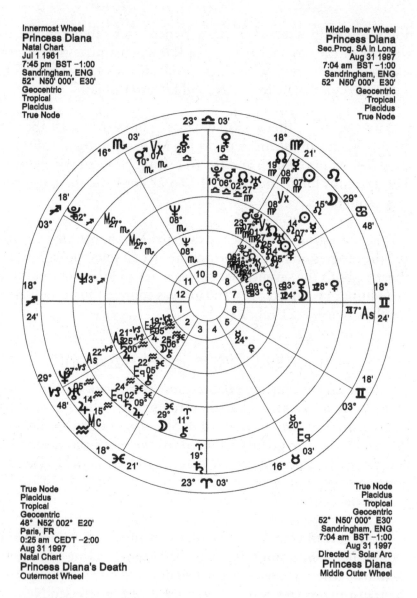

Innermost Wheel
Princess Diana
Natal Chart
Jul 1 1961
7:45 pm BST −1:00
Sandringham, ENG
52° N50' 000° E30'
Geocentric
Tropical
Placidus
True Node

Middle Inner Wheel
Princess Diana
Sec.Prog. SA in Long
Aug 31 1997
7:04 am BST −1:00
Sandringham, ENG
52° N50' 000° E30'
Geocentric
Tropical
Placidus
True Node

True Node
Placidus
Tropical
Geocentric
48° N52' 002° E20'
Paris, FR
0:25 am CEDT −2:00
Aug 31 1997
Natal Chart
Princess Diana's Death
Outermost Wheel

True Node
Placidus
Tropical
Geocentric
52° N50' 000° E30'
Sandringham, ENG
7:04 am BST −1:00
Aug 31 1997
Directed − Solar Arc
Princess Diana
Middle Outer Wheel

and both opposed her natal Vertex in the eighth. Furthermore, the progressed Vertex was conjunct her eighth house Mars, an appropriate signature of a car accident.

7

Conjunctions to the Vertex, AntiVertex, Equatorial Ascendant and the Equatorial Descendant

In the Natal Chart

Vx = Vertex

Av = AntiVertex

Eq = Equatorial Ascendant

Ed = Equatorial Descendant

Kaye Shinker, who has worked with conjunctions to the Vertex, AntiVertex, Equatorial Ascendant and the Equatorial Descendant, offers these possibilities for interpretation (as well as a few ideas of my own):

The last two points have been erroneously called the East Point and West Point. Actually, the Vertex is the West Point (directly west of the place of birth) and the AntiVertex is the East Point (the point directly east of the place of birth). The Equatorial Ascendant is the Ascendant one would have if born at the equator, and the Equatorial Descendant is the Descendant one would have if born there.

She finds that "these points can be clues to minor themes in the horoscope, but if conjunct a natal planet they become major themes in the horoscope, especially if the conjunction is part of a repeated theme."

Sun conjunct Av or Eq

Extreme pride, showmanship and need for applause.

Examples: Oprah Winfrey, O.J. Simpson, and Wynonna Judd

Sun conjunct Vx or Ed

Risk-takers in love, need people who live on the edge, people who can be in charge of others or come before others in the public.

Examples: Lucille Ball, Harry S. Truman, and Ralph Nader

Moon conjunct Av or Eq

Nesting for emotional security, ambivalent over space vs. involvement.

Examples: Patrick Swayze, the Queen Mother, and Harry S. Truman

Moon conjunct Vx or Ed

Attract people who expect to be mothered, strong emotions, and a need to be considerate of the partner.

Examples: Richard Nixon, Monica Lewinsky, and Whoopi Goldburg

Mercury conjunct Av or Ed

They strive to be bright and articulate.

Examples: Donald Trump, Abraham Lincoln, Tony Blair, and Saddam Hussein

Mercury conjunct Vx or Eq

Attract a verbose or extremely intelligent partner, people who take a mental view of life and have well-developed verbal skills.

Examples: Grandma Moses, Donald Rumsfeld, John F. Kennedy, and Fidel Castro

Venus conjunct Av or Eq

Identity focuses on beauty and material pleasures.

Examples: Oprah Winfrey, Johnny Carson, and Bill Bradley

Venus conjunct Vx or Ed

Partners are artistic or materialistic, they seek happy relationships and they want materially prosperous partners.

Examples: George W. Bush, Dick Cheney, Mother Teresa, and Hillary Clinton

Mars conjunct Av or Eq

Vitality and high physical energy.

Examples: Newt Gingrich, Ted Danson, and Sonny Bono

Mars conjunct Vx or Ed

Drawn to aggressive or assertive people, or may be the perennial victim; their careers may necessitate carrying weapons such as policemen.

Examples: Barbara Bush, John F. Kennedy, Prince Charles, and Woody Allen

Jupiter conjunct Av or Eq

A perfectionist or religious zealot.

Examples: Ariel Sharon, Bernadette Peters, Princess Diana, and Bill Clinton

Jupiter conjunct Vx or Ed

The partner expects you to be ideal or perfect; achievements are often high and bring increased status, in some cases, fame.

Examples: Henry Kissinger, Prince Charles, Grace Kelly, and Woodrow Wilson

Saturn conjunct Av or Eq

The father image is the standard for behavior.

Examples: Cecil Rhodes, General Douglas MacArthur, Bill Cosby, and Winston Churchill

Saturn conjunct Vx or Ed

Intense projection of self on significant other, a hard worker who takes life seriously.

Examples: Tony Blair, Anne Marrow Lindburg, and Grandma Moses

Uranus conjunct Av or Eq

Weird, freaky, or humanitarian.

Examples: Ariel Sharon, George W. Bush, Andrew Johnson, and Prince Charles

Uranus conjunct Vx or Ed

Transforms friends into lovers; people who work with technology, or with travel.

Examples: Barbara Walters, Bernadette Peters, and Ghandi

Neptune conjunct Av or Eq

They directly express artistic healing or victim potential.

Examples: Henry David Thoreau, Jack London, and George Bush, Sr.

Neptune conjunct Vx or Ed

They attract Pisces types or garbage collectors; artistic, spiritual, or religious interests; may be attracted to alcohol or drugs.

Examples: Joan Baez, Tony Blair, Paul Newman, Malcolm X, and Adolph Hitler

Pluto conjunct Av or Eq

Obsessive-compulsive self-analysis.

Examples: Woody Allen, Abraham Lincoln, and Lyndon Johnson

Pluto conjunct Vx or Ed

Attract jealous, possessive-compulsive partners; often have control issues from or toward others; can function in large organizations well.

Examples: Pat Boone, Tom Brokaw, Bob Dylan, and Barbara Bush

To some extent, these interpretations can apply to the signs as well, so that the Vertex in Capricorn is somewhat like the Vertex conjunct Saturn or The Vertex in Taurus is somewhat like the Vertex conjunct Venus.

In Synastry

Ties between one person's Vertex or AntiVertex and another person's planets or angles can be very strong. The same is true with charts of businesses or organizations, pets, or any other type of chart as well. These contacts may help explain strong associations between people (or other entities) that otherwise do not seem to be indicated, or they may reinforce those that do have other indications.

A's Vx conjunct B's Sun

They reinforce the feeling of importance each feels. The two may feel they belong in each other's life or would like to be. Although there can be a sense of competition, they can balance each other's self-awareness.

A student of mine says she has this contact with many close important relationships in her life.

A's Vx conjunct B's Moon

One of the two provides nurturing to the other willingly (unless afflicted), and they may feel they are or ought to be part of the same family. It's a strongly emotional relationship.

My beloved French poodle (Vx) and I (Moon) had this contact.

A's Vx conjunct B's Mercury

They encourage each other to express their innermost thoughts, and they influence each other's ways of thinking and expressing themselves. Mentally, they find much agreement.

Princess Margaret (Mercury) and Anthony Armstrong-Jones (Vx)

A's Vx conjunct B's Venus

Unless afflicted there can be much deeply felt affection. This is positive for romantic or any other relationship. There is often agreement in financial and aesthetic matters as well.

Barbara Bush (Vx) and George Bush, Sr. (Venus)

A's Vx conjunct B's Mars

While they motivate each other's actions, especially physical activities, care must be taken to avoid strife since they push each other's buttons. There can be sexual attraction, or they could become rivals or enemies.

Mia Farrow (Mars) and Woody Allen (Vx)

A's Vx conjunct B's Jupiter

The Jupiter individual brings expansion into the Vertex person's life. They both benefit from this association which brings them involvement in the world in which they live. There is trust in each other.

A close friend and a nephew have both had this contact with my Vx. I believe we have expanded each other's lives.

A's Vx conjunct B's Saturn

Often there is an age or social status difference between the two. One may be more experienced in some area making him or her feel like the student and the other the teacher.

Princess Diana (Vx) and Prince Charles (Saturn); Prince Andrew (Vx) and Sara Ferguson (Saturn)

A's Vx Conjunct B's Uranus

This can produce some surprises in a relationship. This is good for friendships where each operates as a unique individual finding him or herself through the association.

Among my friends in astrology, several have Uranus conjunct my Av. I could find none with Uranus conjunct my Vx.

A's Vx conjunct B's Neptune

The tie here can be psychic, religious, or one of mutual idealization. They are highly sensitive to each other, or they may encourage a lack of reality in each other. Mutual interest in the arts is possible too.

Queen Elizabeth II (Neptune) and Prince Philip (Vx)

A's Vx conjunct B's Pluto

These two can transform each other's lives. There is danger that one may feel controlled by the other's urge for power. Sexual attraction may occur. Both learn much about themselves from this association.

Jim Bakker and Tammy Faye Bakker

A's Vx conjunct B's Ascendant

This is a particularly strong contact in family associations or between a person and a business or organization when the person has a strong participation in it.

A personal example is that my mother (Ascendant) and I (Vx) had this contact, a very strong and positive tie.

A's Vx conjunct B's Midheaven

This is found between Burt Reynolds (Midheaven) and Loni Anderson (Vx)

A's Vx conjunct B's Descendant

This is found between John F. Kennedy (Descendant) and Jackie Kennedy Onassis (Vx)

Kaye Shinker gives an example of how these conjunctions work:

> It is a little easier to see in the expression of these conjunctions in long-term relationships.
>
> Someone whose Mars is conjunct your Vertex will make you angry or somehow get you to do work you'd prefer not to do. You mumble and seethe because they said all the right words; they pushed your buttons.
>
> Your father's Mars is conjunct your Vertex and opposed your AntiVertex. You need to work with him, but he inhibits your personal expression by asking for your help when you are working on your own project. No matter how you try to avoid the stimulus, his actions push your buttons and you need to act. Once in a while even though it is hard, you should try to go to the opposite polarity, your AntiVertex. You need to push the Vertex button off and switch on the charm of your Libra AntiVertex. You don't need to growl at Dad—just give him a big hug.

Malefics Conjunct One's Vertex

Expressing the AntiVertex when someone's malefics are conjunct your Vertex may alleviate the negativity of this contact. If your Vertex is in:

Aries: show the charming side of your nature of your Libra AV.

Taurus: show the self-control of your Scorpio AV.

Gemini: express the principles behind the facts of your Sagittarius AV.

Cancer: accept responsibility and function in the outer world like your Capricorn AV.

Leo: show the uniqueness and democratic ideals of your Aquarius AV.

Virgo: demonstrate the faith and compassion of your AV.

Libra: use the initiative and drive of your Aries AV.

Scorpio: express the enjoyment of your senses of your Taurus AV.

Sagittarius: use the concrete facts of your Gemini AV.

Capricorn: nurture and love unconditionally like your Cancer AV.

Aquarius: discriminate and then recognize and appreciate the achievements and values of your Leo AV.

Pisces: express the analytical attitude toward others of your Virgo AV.

Since the Vertex and AntiVertex work like an on and off switch, Kaye Shinker suggests:

If your Vertex is in Taurus and someone pushes your "on" button, your reaction is to flirt or throw them out of the kitchen or force them to sit in a corner. However, you know the way to avoid conflict is to be prim and proper, feed them sweets, or indulge their whim. If your Vertex is in Scorpio, the opposite is true. Sometimes you have to stop controlling others and allow them to push the issue.

If your Vertex is in Sagittarius and you become too abstract and philosophical for people to understand you, switch to the Gemini AntiVertex and give people concrete facts and examples.

8

The Vertex and Solar Returns

When I decided to research the effect of the Vertex in solar returns, it occurred to me that **a good place to start was with my own chart**. Who else would spend the hundreds of hours required to do this? Several years ago I made a notebook with all of my solar returns for the location where I lived most of each year which was usually also my location at the time of each return.

We Cancerians have a mind like a steel trap, especially for events in the early years of our lives, but it also helped to **compile a list of hundreds of the events of all kinds that had occurred in my life** since I was born in 1932. This I did many years ago and added to the list dates as close to the exact time as possible. Sometimes this was the actual date or sometimes just the actual month. Some "events" do not occur on a single day but rather "the spring of 19??" or during some period like that. This list was added to my notebook after I got the dates into chronological order. Every two or three months, I update the list. Other sections were compiled of all the solar returns charts, secondary progressed charts and the solar arc directed charts for each birth date. **This notebook has been invaluable for research.** I encourage all students of astrology to do the same.

The next step was to **identify the years with significant Vertex activity and correlate these with the events of that year. At first I looked only for conjunctions with natal planets and angles. It soon became apparent that these were usually the years of the most significant events in the sense that these events changed the direction of my life in some way. A few were highly significant. Later I looked for oppositions (conjunctions of the Anti-Vertex with natal planets and angles). These were somewhat less significant but usually more personal and not so strongly involved with other people as the Vertex conjunctions.

Finally, I looked for the years with other aspects, the sextile, square, trine and quincunx, to these points. Even these had some significance, but they did not usually change the direction of my life.

There were several **squares** as well as conjunctions to Pluto that indicated drastic changes. For me, that was often a move since Pluto is one of the rulers of the fourth in my chart, however, one of these squares of return Vertex to natal Pluto occurred the year I was diagnosed with cancer and decided to take early retirement from teaching. Furthermore, some of the **quincunxes** also were indicative of health issues or adjustments for other reasons that had to be made.

It became obvious that **conjunctions of return planets to the return Vertex** were also significant according to the nature of the planet, and, in some instances, the house.

For example the return Vertex was conjunct return Neptune in Libra when I returned to college (Neptune rules my ninth house) and studied music (Neptune and Libra—music). In another solar return, the return Ascendant was conjunct the natal Vertex. In the same chart the return Vertex was conjunct return Jupiter and conjunct natal Ascendant and Mercury. These were during the year that I filed for divorce, quit teaching music and started teaching all English classes.

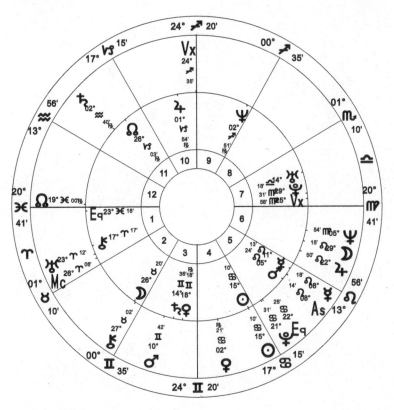

Inner Wheel
Donna Henson
Solar Return
Jul 7 1972 (±3 secs)
0:02:34 am CDT +5:00
Euless, TX
32° N50'13" 097° W04'54"
Geocentric
Tropical
Placidus
True Node

Outer Wheel
Donna Henson
Natal Chart
Jul 7 1932
7:12 am CST +6:00
Kearney, NE
40° N41'58" 099° W04'52"
Geocentric
Tropical
Placidus
True Node

The chart for my 1972 solar return has the return **Midheaven conjunct the natal Vertex** and square the return Vertex. This was the time of perhaps the most traumatic event in my own life which occurred September 3, 1972. Although the final outcome was beneficial, it certainly turned my life permanently upside down. I usually find that an angle to an angle has little significance in itself, but it tends to make other activations at the time more important than one would expect.

Inner Wheel
Princess Diana
Solar Return
Jul 1 1997 (±1 secs)
12:31:22 pm BST −1:00
London, ENG
51° N30' 000° W10'
Geocentric
Tropical
Placidus
True Node

Outer Wheel
Princess Diana
Natal Chart
Jul 1 1961
7:45 pm BST −1:00
Sandringham, ENG
52° N50' 000° E30'
Geocentric
Tropical
Placidus
True Node

A look at the solar returns of people who have been in the news for the years of important events in their lives was the next step. While not all solar returns had significant Vertex activations, enough of them were to justify looking at these charts along with their natal, progressed, directed, and transit charts.

The first one is **Princess Diana's** solar return for the birth date just before her fatal accident on August 31, 1997. She had been in

Paris with the man whom some thought would be her fiancée, Dodi Al-Fayed. The couple had left the Ritz Hotel, owned by Dodi's father and was being driven by a security manager, Henri Paul. The regular chauffeur and vehicle were sent ahead as a decoy for photographers. A chase developed when some photographers on motorcycles realized the ploy. The accident happened in the tunnel.

Analysis of the car accident shows that the Mercedes hit a curb and lost control. The car spun and then hit a concrete barrier post very hard. Then the car flipped several times.

Dodi Al-Fayed and Henri Paul were killed at the scene of the accident. She was brought to a hospital after an extremely long delay where she died. She was pronounced dead at the hospital about four hours after the accident.

The Vertex of the return is a little over two degrees from her Ascendant-Descendant axis opposing Mars and square natal Mercury. There is also a grand trine in the return chart of the Vertex trine Venus in the tenth trine Pluto in the third showing the huge outpouring of grief and love to the Princess from all over the world.

George W. Bush's solar return previous to his election to the Presidency shows his natal Vertex conjunct the return Chiron opposition the return Mercury across the second and eighth houses, the money houses. The return chart ruler, Venus, is in the eighth (support from others) conjunct the return Vertex. It is a ninth house return (where the Sun is) indicating that he would be dealing with the principles of things and foreign matters. Mars, not being angular, shows that he was not in a militant mood at that time. The emphasis on Gemini and Sagittarius show that he (and the rest of the world) is dealing with ideological and religious conflicts.

Dylan Klebold, was the young man who, along with Eric Har-

Inner Wheel
George W. Bush
Solar Return
Jul 5 2001 (±1 secs)
2:21:23 pm EDT +4:00
Washington, DC
38° N53'42" 077° W02'12"
Geocentric
Tropical
Placidus
True Node

Outer Wheel
George W. Bush
Natal Chart
Jul 6 1946
7:26 am EDT +4:00
New Haven, CT
41° N18'29" 072° W55'43"
Geocentric
Tropical
Placidus
True Node

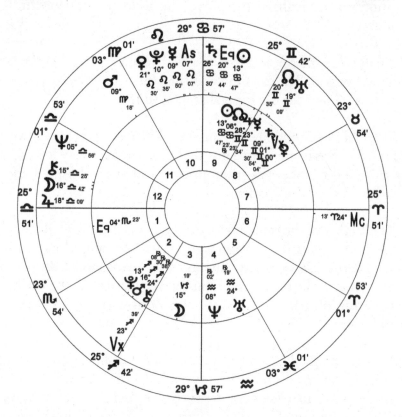

ris, killed 13 students and a teacher at Columbine High School in Littleton, Colorado. On April 20, 1999, a day probably chosen because it was the anniversary of Hitler's birthday, these two gunmen approached the cafeteria at Columbine High School shooting and throwing explosive devices. They continued shooting as they entered the building through the cafeteria. Then they entered the school hallway and went up a stairway to the school library, where they systematically shot students and ultimately killed

Inner Wheel
Dylan Klebold
Solar Return
Sep 11 1998 (±0 secs)
11:45:34 am MDT +6:00
Littleton, CO
39° N36'48" 105° W00'58"
Geocentric
Tropical
Placidus
True Node

Outer Wheel
Dylan Klebold
Natal Chart
Sep 11 1981
9:11 am MDT +6:00
Denver, CO
39° N44'21" 104° W59'03"
Geocentric
Tropical
Placidus
True Node

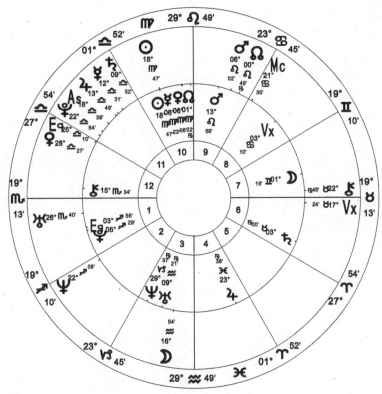

themselves. It is evident that this act was planned long in advance. Within a few minutes of the start of the shooting the first sheriff's deputies arrived. Twenty minutes from the start of the shooting the first members of the swat team arrived on the scene. One hour after the shooting began it ended. Yet, it was not until two hours later that the Swat teams entered the building to evacuate the students, and an hour and a half after they entered the building that they found the bodies of the killers.

Inner Wheel
O.J. Simpson
Solar Return
Jul 8 1995 (±1 secs)
11:13:12 pm PDT +7:00
Los Angeles, CA
34° N03'08" 118° W14'34"
Geocentric
Tropical
Placidus
True Node

Outer Wheel
O.J. Simpson
Natal Chart
Jul 9 1947
8:08 am PST +8:00
Los Angeles, CA
34° N03'08" 118° W14'34"
Geocentric
Tropical
Placidus
True Node

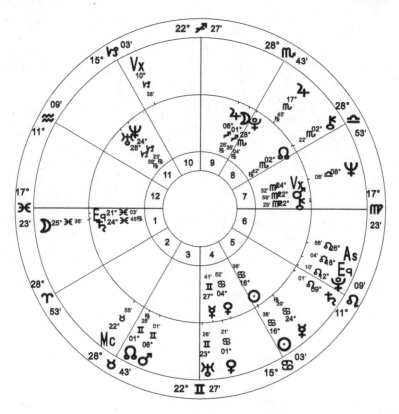

In Klebold's previous solar return, the Equatorial Ascendant (Ep on the chart) is the apex of a yod with Saturn in the sixth and the Vertex in the eighth of death. This Equatorial Ascendant is semi-square his natal Asc. His natal Vertex is less than two degrees from the seventh cusp of the return.

O.J. Simpson was considered to be one of the greatest running backs in football history. He earned All-American honors at the

126

University of Southern California and won the Heisman Trophy as the nation's top college football player in 1968. He set several National Football League records before retiring in 1979. A second career was opening up for him as a sports commentator and actor, but on June 12, 1994 his ex-wife and her friend, Ron Goldman were found murdered at Simpson's Brentwood estate. O. J. was the main suspect in their murders.

After a lengthy trial, he was acquitted October 3, 1995 amid great controversy. Feelings, to a large extent, divided along racial lines with blacks agreeing with the verdict and whites disagreeing. Later in a civil trial brought by the families of Nicole Brown Simpson and Ron Goldman, he was heavily fined and, essentially, found guilty.

His solar return previous to Nicole Simpson's death shows the return Vertex conjunct Mars in the seventh opposing the return Saturn and his natal Moon in the first. This Vertex is trine the return chart ruler, Neptune, in the eleventh, square his natal Uranus in the fourth and sextile natal Mercury in the fifth.

Finally, John F. Kennedy, Jr., who along with his wife, Carolyn Bessette Kennedy and sister-in-law, Lauren Bessette, was killed in an airplane crash July 16, 1999, had some strong indications in his solar return previous to his death. Like Dylan Klebold's return, his has a yod involving the return Vertex in the eighth house. It quincunxes the Sun in the first and Neptune in the third (ruler of the fourth, the end of life) by a little over two degrees. In addition, his natal Vertex is conjunct the return Moon in the third (Moon—women in his life). The yod is one of the classic configurations for a death.

This death of the only son of the 36th U.S. president added to the tragedies experienced by the Kennedy family. We can only wonder what the rest of his life might have been.

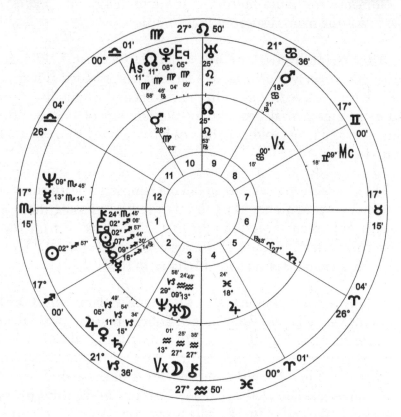

Inner Wheel
John F. Kennedy Jr.
Solar Return
Nov 25 1998 (±1 secs)
5:39:24 am EST +5:00
New York, NY
40° N42'51" 074° W00'23"
Geocentric
Tropical
Placidus
True Node

Outer Wheel
John F. Kennedy Jr.
Natal Chart
Nov 25 1960
0:22 am EST +5:00
Washington, DC
38° N53'42" 077° W02'12"
Geocentric
Tropical
Placidus
True Node

Certainly one does not have significant Vertex activity for the solar returns of every year, but when life-altering events occur, it is often active.

9

Other Uses of the Vertex

Transits of Outer Planets to the Vertex

What little work I have done with transits of outer planets and eclipses to the Vertex has been done mostly with my own chart. I am very fortunate that my birth time was carefully recorded since I am a twin and my twin brother was born an hour and 27 minutes before me. All work with the Vertex is dependent on having accurate birth time.

John Townley wrote of a transit of an outer planet to the Vertex saying, "... a turning point in life is likely to occur with a major transit to the Vertex, *although it may not be recognized as a turning point until long afterward.*" He gave the example of a sexual encounter at the time of such a transit which one realizes only later was significant.

A few examples might illustrate:

t **Jupiter conjunct n Vx** *occurred when I was 4⅓ in the fifth in Sagittarius. I was learning to read then by asking my older brother what a word was and then going through a book I had and underlining that word every time it appeared. Then I asked about a second word and did the same and so on until all the words were underlined.*

Of course this had much significance later and it expanded (Jupiter) my world.

The second time it occurred was when I was 15-16. During this time there was much dating, band trips, and I met my future husband.

The third time was in 1960 when I was in college studying music. I began conducting classes and one of my children started school.

The fourth time I flew to New York City for the first time to spend Christmas with my husband's family.

t Saturn conjunct n Vx *During this time I had a surgery (Saturn is in and rules my sixth), and attended a choir workshop. I remember my energy level being very low.*

t Uranus conjunct n Vx *At this time my mother had to have hip surgeries and was never able to walk again (Uranus in my ninth, her twelfth of hospitalization). My brothers and I went to Houston where she lived every three weeks on a rotating basis. On the positive side, the migraine headaches I'd had for 13 years quit, thanks to three years of acupuncture treatments (with electrical stimulation–Uranus).*

t Neptune conjunct n Vx *The conjunction of Neptune to my Vertex was an eventful time. Its five contacts spanned the time from February 1981 to October 1982. Neptune is in my second in Virgo and it rules the ninth. I met my present husband then and we married at the end of this transit. I also got a Digicomp computer, which was a great help. (The Magi's say Neptune rules computers.) My first book was published (ninth house), we made a long trip to the Northwest and Canada (ninth house), my granddaughter was born (also ninth house), and along with two other women, I opened a bookstore but was unable to continue with it after a short time. Was that ninth house activity or what?*

t Pluto conjunct n Vx *The conjunction of Pluto to my Vertex* *will not occur until 2005, so I can't comment on it yet, but a woman from our astrology group had this transit at the time she married. The couple moved into a home she had been remodeling (Pluto).*

A friend of mine had the transit of Pluto on her Vertex in 1991. It is in her fifth house (children) in Scorpio (loans). She loaned her daughter some money which brought on a rift between them that has not healed to this day.

A neighbor also had this in Scorpio in her fifth and her boyfriend (fifth) of several years died of cancer (Pluto) just about a month before the first contact. During the time of the three contacts she had a very difficult time adjusting to the loss.

George W. Bush will have this transit from January 28, 2005 to November 26, 2005 in Sagittarius in his fifth. It will be interesting to see what he will be dealing with then. Incidentally, on September 11, 2001, transiting Chiron, the wounded healer, was conjunct Bush's Vertex.

Conjunctions to the Anti-Vertex, which are **oppositions** to the Vertex, have been significant too.

t Jupiter conjunct n AV *At age nine, I earned recognition for writing children's stories. At age 21 we got our first television set (Jupiter rules my fifth of entertainment), my son was born (fifth), and at the end of the transit, my grandmother died. We made a long trip for her funeral (Jupiter) where we were reunited with many relatives we hadn't seen for years.*

At age 33 the transit occurred again. We painted and fixed up a new home that we moved in to, and then I worked on my master's degree (Jupiter, natural ninth house ruler).

The next one mapped the time of a very enjoyable astrology convention, followed by a 1989 conjunction when I had cancer and parathyroid surgery (Jupiter in the first—both surgeries were successful).

Finally we had what was almost a vacation while a water leak under our house was repaired. The insurance company put us up in a motel three miles from our home.

t Saturn conjunct n AV *I made my first trip to Europe, but on the plane going there, I got my first migraine headache (Saturn in and ruling the sixth of health). This was the beginning of 13 years of these headaches.*

t Uranus conjunct n AV *This was during my high school years when there was much dating and many band trips. My twin brother and I also bought a motor scooter then delighting our friends and shocking their parents.*

t Neptune and Pluto conjunct n AV *These have not occurred in my lifetime.*

One would expect opportunities to begin something significant from transits which sextile the Vertex.

t Jupiter sextile n Vx *In 1958, I won a creative writing award which gave me more confidence about writing.*

t Saturn sextile n Vx *In 1952, when this occurred, I was taking physical therapy to help recover from polio.*

t Uranus sextile n Vx *I began teaching astrology (Uranus) at the junior college. There was also a trip (Uranus in the ninth) all around the U.S. with a teacher friend, which ended with attendance at an astrology convention in San Francisco.*

t Neptune sextile n Vx *Most of this period was spent in caring for our children and taking care of our home. There were some home-dec-*

orating activities.

t Pluto sextile n Vx *I sold my part of an astrology book store that I had had for a brief time.*

Due to the nature of the aspect, one would expect obstacles that have to be overcome with the **squares**. There have been many of these.

t Jupiter square n Vx *This was when my first son was born (Jupiter rules the fifth of children) He had colic. Another Jupiter transit was during my first year of teaching. I had more to learn than the students did.*

t Saturn square n Vx *This was when I returned to teaching after getting my master's degree. Our overworked counselor failed to sign up a talented accompanist for the chorus class making the year very difficult. Another transit like this was when I had to have a molar extracted because the root had cracked (Saturn—teeth).*

t Uranus square n Vx *This occurred when, at age 35, I filed for divorce (Uranus rules my seventh).*

t Neptune square n Vx *Has not occurred in my chart.*

t Pluto square n Vx *Besides my grandmother's death and the birth of my third son, this was a period in which I began to get active in church, which became very important for the next 10 to 15 years.*

Quincunxes usually indicate the need for adjustments, health concerns, or, in extreme cases, death of someone in the person's life.

t Jupiter quincunx n Vx *Our family moved from Nebraska to Texas after my mother had remarried.*

t Saturn quincunx n Vx *This gave me a glimpse of injustice. I lost out to another girl in being the eighth grade valedictorian since her father was on the school board.*

t Uranus quincunx n Vx *During this time I designed and we built and moved into a new home.*

t Neptune and Pluto quincunx n Vx *I have not had these transits.*

Eclipses to the Vertex

Another area just begging for more research is a study of the effects of solar and lunar eclipses that are conjunct the natal Vertex. I am using an orb of about three degrees, although some astrologers will want to vary this. I have had nine such conjunctions in my life. I can associate a reasonably significant event with each of them.

Since my Vertex is at 24 Sagittarius 35 in the fifth house, all of these would possibly present times when I was completing the gap in my life or personality indicated by the sign and/or house. Themes of learning beyond the usual, church activities, higher education, long distance travel, publishing, and public speaking; in other words, Sagittarius themes-were definitely present.

Following is a list of these nine conjunctions and the events surrounding them:

December 13, 1936–solar eclipse 2 Sagittarius 49, 2°46' from exact

- Learned to read.

- My twin brother and I sang for a women's group.

June 14, 1946–lunar eclipse 23 Sagittarius 03, 1°32' from exact

- Lost out on being eighth grade valedictorian.
- Took lessons in oil painting.

December 14, 1955–solar eclipse 21 Sagittarius 31, 3°04' from exact

- Moved to a new house and a new community where my life opened up through intense activities with the church.

June 14, 1965–lunar eclipse 22 Sagittarius 43, 1°51' from exact

- Decided to move closer to the school where I taught and to take a leave of absence the following year to work on my Masters degree.

June 15, 1973–lunar eclipse 24 Sagittarius 42, 0°07' from exact

- Month-long trip to northern Europe.
- Had first migraine headache.

December 15, 1982–solar eclipse 23 Sagittarius 05, 1°30' from exact

- My book on degrees of the zodiac came out.

June 13, 1984–lunar eclipse 22 Sagittarius 31, 1°59' from exact

- Travel to the eastern part of the U.S.

June 15, 1992–lunar eclipse 24 Sagittarius 24, 0°11' from exact

- Got NCGR to schedule a convention in the Dallas/Fort Worth area.

- Arranged for Doris Greaves to do a workshop in Fort Worth.

December 14, 2001–solar eclipse 22 Sagittarius 56, 1°39' from exact

- Spoke on the Vertex to the Houston NCGR chapter.

- Heard that I was to be nominated to be president of the Astrological Society of Fort Worth.

More research is needed to determine if eclipses on the Vertex primarily activate themes related to the sign of the Vertex. Since many of these events had an element of pleasure, entertainment, or pursuit of hobbies, it is possible the house of the Vertex (fifth) is an indicator too.

Like most eclipse activity, the eclipse seems to intensify experiences, and all of these experiences were indicated in other ways as well.

The Vertex in Financial Astrology

Kaye Shinker graciously permitted me to quote some of her findings on using the Vertex in financial astrology:

In financial astrology the Vertex can indicate the success of an initial public offering of a company's stock. The first day a stock is offered for sale on the New York exchanges is often very critical to the success of that particular equity. We use the time of the opening of the exchange as the time for the event. Most new offerings have buyers lined up several days before the actual selling date. Stock sales begin with the opening bell. Companies that have survived years after their initial public offering have planets making almost exact Ptolemaic aspects to the Vertex.

Examples: American Express did not leave home without Neptune conjunct the Vertex. Mars and Venus are also trine the Vertex.

General Electric brings good things to light with Venus and Neptune making a grand trine that includes the Vertex.

Hershey's Mercury trines its Vertex and the Vertex sextiles its Pluto. I want you to know that that is the astrological explanation as to why their product is fattening.

References

Dewey, Ruth N. "The Vertex-AntiVertex, What It Is and How to Determine It." *The Astrological Review*, Fall 1974, pp. 3-10.

Greaves, Doris. *Regulus Ebertin Cosmobiology Beyond 2000*. Red Hill, ACT 2603, Australia: Regulus Astrological Publications, 1999.

Greaves, Doris. "Vertex and Eastpoint." Lecture notes given at the AFA Convention in Anaheim, June 1994.

Hand, Robert. *Essays on Astrology*. West Chester, PA: Whitford Press, 1982.

Jay, Delphine. "The Third Dimension of Self: the Vertex." *Astrology Now*. II, February 16, 1977, pp. 30-34+.

Reyer, Virginia. "Vertex or Prime Vertical." *Cosmobiology International Journal*. March 1994, pp. 9-10.

Shinker, Kaye. "East Point and Vertex." *Today's Astrologer*. LIV, November 24, 1992, pp. 393-405.

Shinker, Kaye. "East Point, Vertex: Examining the Black Hole Through Synastry." *Welcome to Planet Earth 1994*, pp. 15, 27.

Index

Printed in June 2023
by Rotomail Italia S.p.A., Vignate (MI) - Italy